Coleus

A guide to
cultivation and identification

COLEUS

A GUIDE TO CULTIVATION AND IDENTIFICATION

by

Roy and Kenneth Pedley

THE GARDEN BOOK CLUB
LONDON

Printed and bound in Great Britain by
REDWOOD BURN LIMITED
Trowbridge & Esher

Contents

Foreword   7

Chapter 1
The Ornamental Coleus   9

Chapter 2
Leaf Shapes and Colouring   29

Chapter 3
Botany   42

Chapter 4
Coleus Culture   58

Chapter 5
Towards Perfection   85

Chapter 6
Diseases of Coleus   100

Index   113

Foreword

The ornamental Coleus, like most other popular plants, has undergone considerable change and improvement in recent years. After the geranium it is possibly the most common potted plant to be seen in amateurs' greenhouses and homes.

It is surprising that although ornamental Coleus have been in Europe for about 120 years no comprehensive work has been produced about them, though occasional articles have appeared in horticultural journals from time to time.

Had these plants been regarded as difficult subjects to grow, no doubt more would have been written about them. They are so accommodating and so easily reared that we can become almost contemptuous towards them. Nevertheless, we have come to know that there is as much to learn about Coleus and as much art, creativeness and skill in producing them to perfection, as there is with any other popular plant.

As we accumulated the material for this book, it became obvious that it would be desirable to write not one book but two, the first to be informative and easily read, for the amateur gardener, to be followed by a comprehensive text book on the genus, compiled over a greater number of years. Much information of an academic nature has therefore been withheld from this present work for inclusion in a later one.

7

We write as practising nurserymen and do not claim to have any special knowledge of the sciences and trust that specialists in these subjects will forgive us for anything which may appear naïve.

We acknowledge with gratitude the help given by Pamela, Silve, and Marete with translations. Acknowledgment must also be made to the kindness and efficient help given by County and University Librarians, the British Museum of Natural History, Botany Department, the Royal Horticultural Society and the Royal Botanic Gardens, Kew. We thank also the many other generous-natured people in various parts of the world who, sharing the mutual bond of horticulture, have treated our enquiries with kindness.

I

The Ornamental Coleus

Its origin and background – Arrival in Europe – The Royal Horticultural Society Sales – Coleus fever – Wiliam Bull and his work – The decline – Coleus rehneltianus *– Post-war development.*

The little man and his attendant family paused to admire the display of coleus which we were exhibiting at a flower show. 'Marvellous', he uttered with great feeling. 'Simply marvellous, especially when you realise that these plants have been bred from nettles.' The remainder of his group nodded in agreement and they all shuffled along the aisle in the marquee to the next spectacle.

We often meet people who, like the man above, believe that the coleus is some form of highly developed nettle. One horticultural work that we have, actually asserts this, but it is not so. The stinging nettle is placed in the order URTICACAE and the coleus in LABIATAE. There is no close connection between them botanically.

The terms 'Flame Nettle', 'Painted Nettle' and 'French Nettle' are still in common usage and it is easy to trace how they came about. The coleus is closely allied to Plectranthus and, as we shall see later, any work of this nature must inevitably involve both. One particular plectranthus called *p. fruticosus* was introduced into England from the Cape of Good Hope in 1774. In 1788 L'Heritier published an illustration of it in his '*Stirpes Novae aut Minus Cognitae*'.[1] It shows a plant bearing leaves like a robust plain green coleus. Miller's *Garden Dictionary* of 1808 described it as 'a handsome fragrant plant, with the habit of a nettle.'[2] It became very popular as a window plant, possibly due in some part to its extreme robustness. Hibberd, writing in retrospect in 1869, referred to it as 'of the artisan's window and the plant most frequently seen at any cottagers' and window gardeners' exhibitions.'[3] An article about coleus in *The Gardeners' Chronicle* in May of the same year[4] commented, 'Twenty years ago, almost the only representative of the family was the well known *coleus fruticosus*, the 'Nettle-Leaved Geranium' of our Grandmothers' windows, a plant still sacred in our memory, and admirably adapted for the position it has from time immemorial been called to fill, that of a cottage window adorner. It is essentially a window plant, living and dying there, and never to be seen elsewhere. It cannot lay claim to any merit for beauty either in leaf or flower; it has however an iron constitution, for the more it is mismanaged the better it seems to grow; and it is always green and healthy looking, but nothing more.'

Obviously, the description of these plants as being nettle-like was acceptable. Later on, their multi-coloured-leaved relatives were introduced. As they came into England via the Continent the description 'French Nettle' and 'Flame Nettle' would seem appropriate both to describe their appearance and to distinguish them from the older plain green-leaved types. The term 'Nettle-Leaved Geranium' is puzzling. Possibly 'Geranium' was a term for any window plant loosely applied, but we offer this as a suggestion only.

Many plants of the order Labiatae are highly aromatic. One can recall such plants as Mint, Lavender, Sage, Dead Nettle, Lamium, Thyme and others. Many of the named cultivars of *Coleus blumei* are aromatic, having distinctly different aromas. *C. amboinicus* is used in the South Pacific for scenting oil and to give laundry a pleasant smell.

In central Africa, Ceylon and South East Asia some species of coleus and plectranthus produce tubers which are valuable as a food crop and are cultivated for this purpose. During the summer of 1893 *C. tuberosus* was grown at Kew from tubers imported from Java. In the latter part of the 1950s an attempt was made to grow *C. rotundifolius* as a tuber vegetable crop at Marseilles, but as the soil type was not suitable the attempt was unsuccessful.[5] *C. aromaticus* was reported in 1959 as having pharmacological and anti-bacterial properties useful in the treatment of cholera.[6] In April 1873 *The Gardeners' Chronicle* noted that plectranthus fruticosus was used in Belgium as a window plant in the belief that its presence in the house prevented rheumatism.

The earliest references to coleus are to be found in the works of George Everhard Rumphius. In his *Herbarium amboinensis*, published in 1747, on plate 102, fig. No. 3, we see a single stemmed coleus with variegated leaves. The text matter on page 296 names the specimen *Majana aurea*. Rumphius's life was both energetic and tragic, and he became known later as 'The Pliny of the Indies'. He was born in Hanau, Hessle Cassel, Germany in 1627. After joining the Dutch East India Company he was sent to Batavia in 1653 and settled in Amboina. He took a great interest in the flora of the Indies and by 1670 had almost completed a botanical record. It was his intention to return to Europe to finish it, but he took a final trip to check earlier observations made in the hills. Almost at once he became blind. He carried on with his work, however, aided by his wife and helpers provided for him by the Dutch East India Company. In 1673 he commenced translating his *Herbarium amboinensis* into Dutch but unfortunately in the following year his wife and eldest child were killed in an earthquake. Nevertheless, Rumphius still carried on with his work.

The original illustrations of *Herbarium amboinensis* were made by Rumphius himself before he lost his sight, and on January 11th 1687, these were mostly destroyed in a fire which swept through the area where he lived, burning his house and library. Still determined to continue he persevered with his task

11

aided by his son, T. A. Rumphius, until his death in 1702.[8]

At the suggestion of the American botanist, E. D. Merrill, Dr. Charles Budd Robinson went to Amboina in 1913 to interpret the species described by Rumphius. Unfortunately, owing to a local superstition some natives mistook Dr. Robinson for a mythical personality known as Potong Capala (the decapitator) who, it was believed, wandered about at that particular time of the year with the intention of cutting off people's heads, so they promptly murdered him. Feeling responsible for Dr. Robinson's death, E. D. Merrill went to Amboina and completed the work himself, the translation being published in 1917.[9] On page 460 of this work E. D. Merrill comments upon Rumphius's description of *Majana aurea* stating ' The form described is one of the common cultivated types of coleus with variegated leaves commonly known as *C. blumei benth* . . .' It will be noticed that it is described as ' common cultivated '; we must bear this important fact in mind when considering the development of the coleus. We tend to think of new kinds of plants being brought home by plant hunters, as likely as not from some exciting and almost inaccessible situation, but it was not so with the coleus. There is no doubt that the first living tissue introduced into Europe had been in cultivation in Java for some considerable time. When studying herbarium specimens of these plants one often sees comments such as ' cultivated form ' or ' grown in gardens ' attached. The Kew herbarium contains a very pretty specimen of *C. pumilus Blanco* with an accompanying letter from the sender in Baw, Sarawak, requesting identification because it was so attractive and a suitable candidate for cultivation.

There is an interesting passage in the Journal of the Royal Horticultural Society 1912/13[10] in an article by Sir Everard Imm Thurn headed ' Plant Life in a Tropical Island '. He states, ' I wish I had time here to tell of the many plants cultivated by the natives among the mountains, some for use and some for ornament . . . about the garden varieties of fruits, for use, and plants (forms of Dracaena, Croton, Pandanus and Coleus), which these South Sea natives seem to have developed for their own use and

Coleus Fantasia
White Fern

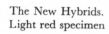

The New Hybrids.
Light red specimen

The New Hybrids.
Warm red specimen

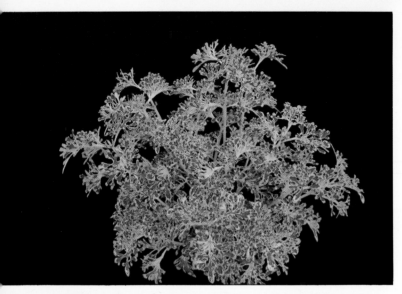

Friendship. A Fantasia type with a bushy, many-fingered
form of leaf.

An attractive composition from the seed-grown stra
'The New Hybrids'.

Coleus Firebrand. A nicely grown standard in a six inch
pot. This specimen is in its second season and is about
sixteen months old.

pleasure, presumably by some process of " selection ", intentional or unintentional, before contact with the folk from the West.' This last point reflects the remarks of Morren[31] in 1880, ' . . . the *Coleus blumei* is not known as a native of Java, but only as cultivated in the gardens of this Dutch Colony. The native country of the species and the origin of its varieties are, then, doubtful questions.' Rumphius described his *Majana aurea* as bearing leaves more pointed than round, being beautiful gold in colour with a large blood-red mark in the centre. He recorded that it was brought to Amboina about the year 1663 from the village of Canaria in Ceram and that it also grew abundantly in the Island of Ternate in the Moluccas.

L. H. Bailey in his *Standard Cyclopaedia of Horticulture* offers the following remarks under *Coleus blumei*. ' This species, founded on cultivated plants in Java, is probably to be regarded as now understood to be an assemblage or combination of species. The horticultural forms are perhaps derived in part . . . from *C. laciniatus*, *C. bicolor*, and perhaps they are to be considered also in connection with *C. atropurpureus* Benth. of Malaysia and its relatives.'

Plectranthus fruticosus, as we said earlier, soon established itself as a popular window plant. From time to time, other closely related plants were introduced and noted in horticultural books. One such was *Ocimum scutellarioides* which was collected on the island of Tanna. A picture of this plant appeared in Curtis's *Botanical Magazine* in 1812,[11] along with a description. The writer reiterated earlier botanists' remarks that the complex including these families of plants should be re-examined, as minute technical differences in their flowers were causing difficulty to botanists. (This is still the case but we will raise this in a different chapter.) In 1826 the botanist Blume mentioned *Plectranthus scutellarioides*, describing it as being spotted above with dark purple (*folia supra maculis atro-purpureis picta*) and that it was cultivated.[12] When Bentham produced his *Genera & Species Labiate* (1832/36) he classed this plant as *Coleus blumei*[13] and it was under this name that it was introduced into Europe. The man who had the pleasure of this event was M. J. A. Willink who introduced it into Amsterdam in 1851. The event was published in *Flore des Serres*, 1852.[14] The plant eventually reached England and in 1853 a description, together with a coloured illustration was shown in Curtis's *Botanical Magazine*.[15] The text includes the comment '. . . we are indebted for our first knowledge of this plant in a living state to Mr. Low of Clapton Nursery, who received the plant from Belgium, as a native from Java; but even there, Blume speaks of it only as cultivated in gardens. As such it is an extremely ornamental plant, the leaves being intensely mottled and blotched with deep purple or sanguineous stains. . . .'

The illustration showed a shoot bearing seven or eight leaves and terminating in a flower spike. The leaves might be described as being like an elongated nettle, serrated with well defined saw-toothed edges. Most of the leaf centre was coloured purple and red, the edges of the leaf being green. The leaf blade was attenuated towards the petiole and rhomboidal ovate in shape. This distinctive feature is still to be seen in many of the cultivated coleus of the present day. Three years later in 1856 Morren[16] reported the existence of *C. blumei pectinatus*. The illustration shows a plant with leaves much more deeply serrated than those of the type first introduced. Some of the segments of the serrations were themselves serrated, resembling fleur-de-lis.

In 1861 a different coloured coleus was introduced and the circumstances were later reported by Morren in 1880,[17] '. . . Captain Mammes took it back in 1860, from Java, to the Botanical Garden of Rotterdam; it began to circulate among the Dutch horticulturalists, but very modestly, when it was noticed by M. Ambroise Verschaffelt, who made the acquisition of it and published it in his *Illustration Horticole* with a description by M. Charles Lemaire . . . the plant was successful and circulated everywhere.'[17] *L'Illustration Horticole* described it as being more vigorous than *C. blumei* with the habit more erect. The leaves were much larger than *C. blumei* and had wavy edges instead of being saw-toothed. The base of the leaves was not attenuated but was more square with the petiole, or even 'heart-ear' shaped. The plants' stems were described as being purple just like the foliage. M. Lemaire named this *Coleus verschaffeltii*.

The Gardeners' Chronicle of June 8th 1861 reported the Grand Flower and Fruit Show held by the Royal Horticultural Society on the 5th and 6th of the same month. This stated that 'There was from M. Jean Verschaffelt a *Coleus verschaffeltii* from Java, a plant like the common coleus, but with leaves almost wholly empurpled.' Eight months later in February 1862 the same periodical had an article encouraging gardeners to cultivate this new plant stating ' That this is a first rate plant of its kind I think all will admit who have seen it grown.'

Floral Magazine of 1862[18] also gave an enthusiastic account of this plant explaining that it was introduced into England by Mr. William Bull, Nurseryman, of King's Road, Chelsea. It was exhibited by him at the various horticultural exhibitions in the metropolis during the previous season attracting considerable attention. The foliage was described as being ' elegant in shape, and on the young plants deep crimson, margined with bright green, but as the plants attain age and size the green passes away, and the entire leaf is a rich glowing crimson; in this condition they are very beautiful, having a velvety appearance . . . .' A footnote included the comment that the Royal Horticultural Society was about to try it.

At the Flower Show held in Regent's Park in May of 1864 a sport of *C. verschaffeltii* was exhibited as a new plant. It had bright green patches on its leaves and it was claimed to be hardier than the parent. A cautious comment in the *The Gardeners' Chronicle*[19] offered the opinion that although the foliage was enlivened by the intermixture of green, it was not so rich looking as the original.

At about this time Mr. John G. Veitch made a tour of the South Pacific and one result of this was the introduction of two fresh kinds of coleus in 1868. Both were illustrated and described in *Floral Magazine*.[20] The first, which he named *C. gibsonii*, was discovered growing in New Caledonia in vast quantities. Its habit

15

was described as being dwarf and bushy with leaves of light green colour, distinctly veined and blotched with dark crimson purple. The second one was named *C. veitchii* and ' . . . had almost heart-shaped leaves of a deep chocolate colour, with the edges a bright lively green.' The illustration showed the plant having broad heart-shaped leaves which were flat and held in a horizontal plane. The crenations were very shallow, being little more than a slight wavy edge.

During the fifteen years which had elapsed since the introduction of *C. blumei,* both *C. blumei* and *C. verschaffeltii* had become firm favourites as stove plants, decorative plants and summer bedding plants, but no-one could possibly have imagined what was about to happen in the horticultural world as a result of Mr. Veitch's introduction. The greenhouse plant breeders of mid-Victorian England became instantly involved with great enthusiasm, excitement rose to a high pitch and the great Coleus Race was on!

The year of 1868 was notable as one in which the greatest advances were made. Some idea of the interest and enthusiasm aroused can be gained from an article written by Shirley Hibberd in *New, Rare and Beautiful Leaved Plants* in 1869. ' It was to be expected that a plant so famous for its uses in ornamental gardening should be taken in hand by the hybridists. This, indeed, has been the case to such an extent, that at the time of writing this note the horticultural world may be said to be in a Coleus fever. The most successful hybridist is Mr. Bause, in the service of the Royal Horticultural Society at Chiswick, the raiser of a number of varieties, several of which are of the highest merit.'

Mr. F. Bause worked with *C. blumei*; *C. verschaffeltii*; *C. gibsonii* and *C. veitchii* and quickly achieved some positive results. On Tuesday, April 7th 1868 a selection of the new forms was exhibited at a meeting of the Royal Horticultural Society's Floral Committee at South Kensington. These created considerable interest and *The Gardeners' Chronicle* of April 11th reported this showing in detail, giving a full description of twelve named types together with details of their crosses. In every instance *C.*

verschaffeltii was the seed parent. Of the twelve crosses made, the pollen parents were *C. veitchii* six, *C. gibsonii* five and *C. blumei* one. The different leaf forms indicated that true crosses had been effected.

The same issue of *The Gardeners' Chronicle* also published an announcement which ran as follows: 'We are requested to announce that the Council of the Royal Horticultural Society has determined to offer to public competition, by auction, at STEVENS'S Rooms, the splendid collection of twelve NEW HYBRIDS of COLEUS raised in the Society's Garden, and of which descriptions will be found in another column. The sale will take place on Wednesday, the 22nd inst. This step has been wisely adopted for the purpose of allowing these valuable novelties to be speedily distributed by the trade throughout the country, so that the public generally may be able to acquire and enjoy a set of the finest decorative plants which have recently been obtained.'

The sale of the twelve plants realised the astonishing grand total of £390, the highest figure being given by Messrs. Veitch & Sons for the plant of *C. bauseii* which was sold for 59 guineas. This firm bought six of the twelve plants in all. Messrs. Carter bought four and Mr. Wills the remaining two. The new owners lost no time in advertising their acquisitions and on May 2nd *The Gardeners' Chronicle* displayed (on page 458) advertisements by two firms offering between them eight of the twelve kinds. Both firms claimed to have varieties described as either 'The finest and most distinct' or 'of the most distinct and beautiful'. Prices ranged between 10/6d ($1.30) and 15/– ($1.95) each, the plants to be supplied from June 1st and during the ensuing summer.

Another advertisement on the same page featured the first release to the public of a golden yellow sport of *C. blumei* named *Coleus telfordi (aurea)*, also priced at 10/6d ($1.30) each. There is no account of any interest by Mr. Wm. Bull of Chelsea (who introduced *C. verschaffeltii* into Britain) in the sale of the twelve Chiswick hybrids. An advertisement by him on the same page indicates a possible reason, why, for interplaced between the two major announcements is one by William Bull, F.L.S. offering a collection of eighteen different sorts of his own breeding. The advertisement stated that Mr. Bull had raised by careful fertilisation upwards of one hundred and fifty beautiful new varieties, of which the above (eighteen) had been selected to be put into commerce. A vivid and colourful description of them followed, together with a reminder of their utility for all types of decoration. He further assured readers that the merits of the varieties he was offering could scarcely be over-estimated and that he would be happy to show these new hybrids to visitors to his establishment.

The writings of this period give clear indication of the fever and excitement accompanying the development of these new and colourful plants. Inevitably too, something of the character of those involved shows through the accounts of their work. Of these, one cannot avoid being impressed by the personality of Mr. Bull. He was a fellow of the Linnaean Society; his catalogues indicate that he must have possessed very considerable skill and knowledge in his profession. His business sense and acumen was unquestionable; in the timing of his releases he appears to have gained from others' publicity.

When Mr. Bull introduced *C. verschaffeltii* into England, he exhibited it throughout the summer of 1861, following A. Verschaffelt's showing of it in June of that year. His catalogue for 1867 offered stock of both *C. gibsonii* and *C. veitchii*, this being the season immediately following Veitch's description of them. There is no doubt that Mr. Bull would use both of these types for breeding purposes during 1867 and would be keeping up with Mr. Bause at Chiswick. 'C. B.' reported Mr. Bull's varieties in *The Gardeners' Chronicle* on May 1st 1869 stating '. . . many of which, however, proved identical to the Society's lot though some of them were distinct and good.'[21]

The season of 1868 progressed and with the arrival of November it could have been assumed with confidence that no more sensational developments would be seen that year. But this was not to be the case for the Royal Horticultural Society announced a second sale of hybrids raised by Mr. Bause, to be offered for

sale at STEVENS'S Rooms on December 10th. *The Gardeners'
Chronicle*[22] commented upon these new hybrids with its usual
rapture, ' If the public is not to be sated with new coleuses, there
is now a *bonne bouche* in store for it in the shape of a group of
splendid crimson and gold varieties, which have been raised at
Chiswick during the past summer.' The article then described
many of the varieties in detail, along with their names.

At this crucial moment, while the horticultural world was
stimulated by this recent news, Mr. Bull made an announcement
in the next issue of *The Gardeners' Chronicle*[23] which was published ten days before the announced date of the second sale.
The content of the advertisement must have come as a surprise to
many for he offered a wide selection of coleus seed for sale. The
announcement was of considerable length and was headed
' Special Offer of Coleus Seeds ' and went on, ' These seeds may
all be expected to produce very magnificent and distinct new
sorts. . . .' Much of his advertisement read like a Gilbertian description of some horticultural Utopian dream. It stated the origin
of the seed stock and suggested in detail what might be expected
by raising the seed. The descriptions were vivid and exciting and
he emphasised their virtue and utility for ornamental, bedding and
decorative uses. After reminding the public of the ease with which
the plants could be grown and assuring them that the plants'
merits could scarcely be overestimated, he listed a collection of
twenty crosses. The seed offered could be bought separately,
priced at 3/6d (43c) for one seed or 7/6d (95c) for three seeds,
with reductions for collections of larger quantities.

The second sale of Chiswick hybrids was held as arranged on
December 10th but the prices were not as sensational as those of
the previous April. It was briefly reported that ' In consequence
of the market being overstocked with so many varieties, the result
was not favourable from a pecuniary point of view as on the
previous occasion, the sale realising only 65 guineas.'[24] Most of
the purchases went to Messrs. Carter & Co.

Some of the second lot of Chiswick Hybrids had yellow in their
pigmentation and one named Queen Victoria was featured as a

coloured plate on the frontispiece of *The Florist & Pomologist* for 1869. The appearance of yellow in hybrid coleus added to their brightness and variety of colouring. It will be remembered however that a yellow sport named *C. telfordii* aurea had been offered in the previous April. It was originally observed as a sport by Mr. McPhail, gardener to C. Telford Esq., of Bromley, Kent, who noticed that one half of a leaf had sported a golden tint. The axillary bud was rooted and the variety fixed.

It would not be true to say that everyone in the horticultural world was swept along by the 'Coleus Fever'. In 1869, Mr. Shirley Hibberd who used this term in his article 'New Varieties of Coleus' previously mentioned, referred to an illustration of *C. murrayii*, *C. marshallii* and *C. telfordii* with the comment, 'The three leaves figured represent fashionable weeds, beautiful, useful, interesting; nevertheless weeds which in a few years hence will probably be utterly valueless and perhaps unknown. . . . Let us go back, then, to a few elementary facts, so as to bring these new varieties of coleus before our readers as having a place in history and many uses in art, weeds as they are, and from a certain eclectic point of view comparatively valueless. Coleus and plectranthus are two closely allied genera of labiatae. We may speak of them in a homely way as tropical nettles and . . . their affinity with nettles is declared by their looks.' His article went on to mention the work of Mr. Bause and Mr. Bull and ventured the opinion that 'The number of varieties registered as candidates for public favour cannot now be less than fifty.' He then listed eight varieties which he considered as being amongst the most distinct and attractive.

The Gardeners' Chronicle of May 1st 1869, reviewing the period rather more enthusiastically, stated 'Few groups of plants have so rapidly emerged from comparative obscurity into prominence and notoriety as that of the Coleus. . . . The advance was so great, and so little expected, that the country was, as it were, taken by storm by them; and on their being sold (the Chiswick Hybrids) were very speedily to be found in every garden in the country. . . . What are we, however, to expect from the many lovely gems, the second batch of seedlings raised at Chiswick, and now being distributed by several of our leading nurserymen? Here there is colour, and to spare – colour more bright, more rich and deep than the greatest enthusiasts could ever have imagined to belong to foliage. We look for such colours only in flowers. What may not be done with these fine plants when once they are amongst us? For the decoration of our conservatories, and even, windows in winter, flowers, as far as regards colour, may almost be dispensed with.'

In 1869 a French sport of *C. veitchii* was shown at the Royal Horticultural Society on June 1st. This had flat leaves, beautifully marked with red, white and chocolate and was named *C. saisonii*.[25] In 1871 Capt. R. Tryon of Loddington Hall, Leicester, raised a coleus of unusual attractiveness; the leaves were broad and flat with slightly serrated edges. The colorations were not patterned in relation to the length of the leaf but were across it. The upper half of the leaf was maroon, and the lower half golden. A coloured plate of this was shown in *Floral Magazine* 1872,[26] but no mention is made of it later, the form apparently becoming lost.

The notes accompanying the illustration contain an interesting comment which noted an abatement in the 'Coleus Fever'; speaking of the situation in general, it continues, 'Although the great rage has subsided, and the very extravagant prices then given can never be looked for again, they are still much used for these purposes, and nothing can be more beautiful. . . .' During this period the coleus was used extensively throughout Europe as a stove and conservatory plant, for interior decoration in general, and for summer bedding displays where the climate permitted. They were often planted to great effect by Mr. Gibson of Battersea Park, who used them with such skill that they were one of the sights to see, horticulturists often travelling hundreds of miles to see the display. Mr. Gibson planted them out, established in pots, plunging them *en masse* to great effect. If the weather was inclement or the soil cold or wet, however, they did not grow well. It was reported that 'in Derbyshire at Chatsworth, the coleus is useless '.[27]

Throughout the 1870s fresh varieties continued to be offered and interest maintained, but the attitude of both the nursery trade and the gardening public was kept to a more reasonable proportion. Breeding was carried out in Britain and also on the Continent.

Gartenflora in 1878 stated that breeding had been done in Germany at the gardens of E. Benary where new forms with gold, dark purple and green variegated leaves had been raised. At the Paris Exhibition of 1879, Morlet exhibited coleus described as '... surpassing all previous varieties. These had enormous foliage, with remarkable combinations of shades of carmine, yellow and green.'[28]

In 1877 William Bull introduced *C. pictus* from Duke of York Island. This was very bizarre in appearance. The leaf was longer in proportion to its breadth than most other sorts. The coloration was a mixture of yellow and brown, being laid on the leaf in an irregular fashion. The serrations were deeply cut and large, giving the plant a fern-like appearance. The illustration shown in his catalogue for 1877 was reproduced in *Gartenflora* xxvii p. 51 in 1878.

In the following year Mr. Bull introduced two more kinds from the South Pacific. These became named later as Distinction and Surprise. The former had deeply cut leaf segments; the colouring being purple, violet and crimson, with a creamy yellow centre. The latter variety was bright green with a creamy yellow centre.

Mr. Bull had raised many fine varieties but a group of new kinds offered in his catalogue for 1880 surpassed all of his previous breeding. They were distinctly different from earlier forms and set a new high standard. Some were deeply laciniated, with segments cut almost to the mid vein. Others were beautifully frilled and edged. Their colours were strong and intense and included crimson, yellow, white, maroon and green; all were multi-coloured. Their designs were feathered and veined with great beauty. Five varieties were illustrated and upon comparing these against others in various books of the same period there is no doubt about their excellence. These new forms were reported in

The Gardeners' Chronicle[29] receiving the highest praise.

Towards the close of the Victorian era new varieties became less sensational; the coleus was accepted as a plant from a previous generation. They were no longer novel. The coleus fever was spent.

In 1914 the American, A. B. Stout, spent six weeks in Europe investigating the coleus situation. He wrote ' at the present time it does not appear that any pure strains of *C. blumei, C. gibsonii* or *C. veitchii* are in cultivation . . . only one plant – a plant observed in the Royal Botanic Gardens at Regent's Park, London . . . was seen which had the Blumei type of leaf. *C. verschaffeltii* is, however, quite generally in cultivation at the present time and agrees quite closely with the first type described.'[30] Mr. Stout also mentioned a letter sent to him from the Director of 's Lands Plententuin at Buitenzorg, Java, stating, ' *C. blumei,* as figured in *Curtis's Botanical Magazine* is at present not represented here.'

Included in Mr. Stout's report was part of a letter sent to Mr. Chittenden, Secretary of the Royal Horticultural Society, from Mr. B. Wynne, who spent three months of his time as a student at Chiswick under Mr. Bause in the propagating department. He was quite familiar with the methods used in the development of hybrid coleus and stated, ' It fell to my lot to convey the first half-dozen coleuses to Stevens's Rooms.' Mr. Wynne went on ' . . . I am unable to say whether there is more than one of the Chiswick set of coleus in existence now, but I very much doubt it.' The one variety referred to was Queen Victoria, supposedly being marketed under another name. As Mr. Wynne's description differed from the coloured plate in *The Florist & Pomologist*, 1869, Mr. Stout doubted if the variety of which Mr. Wynne spoke was the authentic original variety.

From the turn of the century the standard of quality of coleus tended to decline, no doubt due partly to the fact that more plants were being grown from seed rather than from choice, named cultivars. In 1902 the Royal Horticultural Society reported a trial which included coleus grown from seed and commented, ' . . . but the leaves are rather dull in colour.' It is interesting to note that from the period 1905 to 1934 coleus occur only four times in the index of *The Gardeners' Chronicle*, twice reporting *C. thyrsoideus* and twice describing plants raised from seed. A number of inter-acting factors contributed to the changing scene which affected the fashion in coleus culture and the nature of the plants. The decline in the number of gentlemen's households serving as patrons to horticulture would certainly have its effect. Coleus being used mainly for summer decorative plants had to be kept over winter in heated quarters for stock purposes when grown in the traditional way from cuttings. By sowing seed each early spring the cost of over-wintering was avoided. This method, how-ever, tended to produce smaller sized plants in smaller pots, the public becoming unaware of what a coleus plant in fine stature could attain to.

Plants thus raised tended to run to flower and lose their attrac-tiveness much sooner than named cultivars of earlier days. Gardeners naturally tended to cherish and rear many drab seed-lings which should have been rejected. Many of the named beautiful old varieties flowered late in the season and some not every summer. The best kinds had been released for introduction only when they had proved their merits. The seed method of growing tended to reverse this situation.

When a coleus shoot terminates in a flower spike the develop-ment of further leaves and growing points is thereby frustrated; when the main shoot produces a flower spike after only a few pairs of leaves, the future development and stature of the plant as a thing of beauty is severely limited. The breeding of seed types naturally had to be done with those plants which produced seed with certainty, but the development of a decorative foliage coleus type out of consideration for its seed crop can only hasten its deterioration and ultimate disfavour. Seed production also affected a deterioration in leaf types, producing a standard simple leaf; as mentioned in another chapter, factors carrying the more elegant and delicate features are recessive and quickly submerge, producing a more or less standard type. There is no doubt that by the 1930s few among the gardening public were aware of the beauty of the coleus of earlier years.

During the early years of the 1920s a quite different form of horticultural coleus began to circulate amongst the gardens of Europe. It was named *C. rehneltianus*. A full account of its origin was published in *Botanical Magazine* 1924, no. 9034, together with a plate. According to this we learn that the plant was collected by Herr F. Rehnelt, curator of the Botanic Gardens at Giessen, Hesse. He discovered it in 1914 growing in the neighbourhood of Anuradhapura, the ruined ancient capital of Ceylon It was later named *C. rehneltianus* by Herr A. Berger and distributed by the firm of Haage and Schmidt of Erfurt.

Specimens grown at Kew from seed obtained from Haage and Schmidt were compared against herbarium material collected by Vidal, Loer and Merrill in the Philippines and by Mr. W. H. Smith at Bau in Sarawak (mentioned earlier). The plant appeared to be identical. Some of the earlier specimens had been collected as cultivated plants and others in a wild state.

Botanical Magazine believed *C. rehneltianus* to be identical with *C. pumilus* recorded by the Augustinian monk, Manuel Blanco who lived most of his life in the Philippines. He described a coleus being grown in pots in Manila on account of its quaintly blotched leaves whilst nearby it grew on the tiled roofs of the village of Pasig. The same plant appears to have been reported by Charles Gaudichaud in 1837. Both *Gartenflora* 75: 1926, pp. 360-361, and *Revue Horticole* 1928-29, p. 180, published articles showing illustrations.

The plant had a low, scrambling habit, frequently rooting where the trailing stems touched the earth. It seldom reached more than 25 cms. in height. The leaves on the main stems were about 2 or 3 cms. across and heart-shaped with rounded shallow serrations on each side. The illustration in *Botanical Magazine* showed broadly ovate deltoid leaves generally with five dentations on each side of the leaf. (*C. pumilus blanco* in the Herbarium at the British Museum collected in the forest at Hainan in 1933 has nine crenations.) The centre of the leaf had a dark brownish

25

or blackish-purple area shading out to lighter shades and a bright green edge. At the junction of the petiole and the leaf blade there was a small creamy white area.

Two forms of this plant in general cultivation were grown by us from about 1946 onwards. One popular form known as Lord Falmouth was very successful as a potted plant but it was, in our opinion, too green. The other, known as Picturatum closely resembled the plant described in *Botanical Magazine* but it proved to be rather delicate in constitution and too eager to run to flower. After several years of seeding and re-selection we introduced two new forms possessing brighter colouring. One was named Rob Roy; this had bright red leaf centres with a brown and green edge. The other was named Dunedin and had similar colouring to the former but with a pale yellow stippling. Both of these varieties proved to resemble *C. rehneltianus* in performance as a winter flowering ornamental plant, flowering very well as a basket and a hanging plant.

In 1946 the writers became interested commercially in coleus plant production. Bought seed proved disappointing, colours were drab and poor, there was also considerable uniformity of type and there was a high rejection percentage. These features made commercial production of plants too speculative and motivated our decision to breed our own seed. Over a few seasons it was comparatively easy to improve the colour range and patterns and to develop seeds which produced plants bearing up to ten pairs of leaves before initiating a flower spike. By line breeding, some types produced a fairly uniform progeny.

Crosses were made between our new seedlings and pollen from several flowering plants of old coleus cultivars growing in the same glasshouse. Some of the resulting seedlings were frilled, some laciniated and some had colour patterns quite different from any which we had seen hitherto. Encouraged by this development we continued to use some of these old varieties as pollen parents, breeding into our hybrids many of the features seen only in the named cultivars, some of which dated from the late Victorian era. By the late 1950s this strain had become recognised not only for its colourings but also for the different shapes of the leaves that it produced, e.g. beautifully frilled and laciniated types, strap leaves and pennant shapes, wavy Verschaffeltii edges, Blumei-attenuated leaf blades, *C. pumilus* type leaves and habit in different colours. These forms bred and interchanged their prominent features in bewildering combinations. There were strap leaves which were also frilly, Verschaffeltii types which were also laciniated and so on. Expressed throughout many of these forms was the anastomose veination described in the next chapter. The strain was ultimately named 'The New Hybrids' and has been kept up to date by the inclusion of improved and new forms as they have become available.

Other strains are well known by both the nursery trade and the amateur grower. The popular 'Rainbow Hybrids' produces a uniform type of plant, attaining a height of about 40 cms. when grown in an 11 cm. pot. The colours range over pink, salmon, red, brown and white. Another well known strain is 'Monarch'. This also produces plants which are uniform in shape and type, growing to about 30 cms. high in an 11 cm. pot. The leaves are heart-shaped and held almost horizontal. The leaf patterns are uniform and the colours range over red, pink, bronze, rose and brown.

'Prize Strain' is another well known type containing a wide range of colours. In common with the preceding two strains the leaf forms are in general of a standard uniform shape and pattern.

Most of the well known strains of seed are available in separate colours. Other types and species (or so called species) which have been introduced into horticulture are described in a later chapter.

1 L'Heritier, *Stirpes Novae aut Minus Cognitae, fasc.* iv, 85, t 41. 1788
2 *Millers Garden Dictionary* 1808
3 Hibberd, *New, Rare and Beautiful leaved plants* 1869. p. 89
4 *Gardeners' Chronicle*, May 1st 1869. p. 474
5 *Field Crop Abstracts.* Vol. 31. p. 639
6 *Science and Culture*, 1958, 24 : pp. 241-3

8 *Biographian von Rumphius* (Rouff and Müller)
9 *An Interpretation of Rumphius's Herbarium Amboinense.* E. D. Merrill
10 *Journal of Royal Horticultural Society.* 1912/13, p. 7
11 *Curtis' Botanical Magazine,* 1812. 1446
12 *Blume. Bijdragen tot de Flora van Nederlandsch Indie.* 1826. Vol. III. p. 837
13 Bentham. Genera and Species Labiate, p. 56
14 *Flore des Serres* 1852/53. Ser. I viii; t 801
15 *Curtis's Botanical Magazine,* 1853; 4754
16 Morren, *La Belgique Horticole* 1856, p. 99
17 *L'Illustration Horticole* viii; 293 1861 and *Belgique Horticole* 1880
18 *Floral Magazine* 1862. Pl. 96
19 *Gardeners' Chronicle.* May 28th 1864. p. 506
20 *Floral Magazine* 1867, iv. Pl. 338 and 345
21 *Gardeners Chronicle* May 1st 1869, p. 474
22 "   "   Nov. 21st 1868. p. 1210
23 "   "   Nov. 28th 1868. p. 1232
24 "   "   Dec. 12th 1868. p. 1286
25 "   "   June 5th 1869. p. 616 and *Horticulteur Francaise.* 1870-71, Pl. 4. p. 122
26 *Floral Magazine,* 1872, Pl. 34 and *Gardeners' Chronicle* 1871, pp. 1009 and 1519
27 *Gardeners' Chronicle,* 1865, Sept. 23rd, p. 891
28 Stout, *Journal New York Botanical Garden,* 1916. Vol. xvii, p. 213
29 *Gardeners' Chronicle,* August 28th, 1880 p. 279
30 Stout, *Journal New York Botanical Garden,* 1916, Vol. xvii, pp. 209-218
31 Morren, *Belgique Horticole,* 1880, p. 75

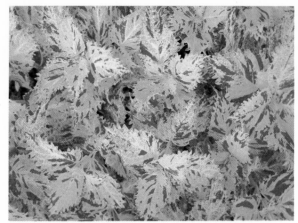

Pixie. A cultivar which can produce specimens of out-standing charm. Of medium vigour and during the winter requiring a temperature a little higher than most other sorts.

Rustic Splendour. A selection of D. T. Brown & Co. Ltd.

Scarlet Ribbons. An excellent, pennant-leaved cultivar. Makes a very bushy plant of good constitution.

Kentish Fire. One of the oldest cuttings-grown cultivars.
Bushy and of medium vigour.

Klondike. A cultivar of excellent colour.

Three good subjects for training into standards. Note t[
strong, straight, sturdy stems. On the left, Lemondro[
in the centre, Firebrand, and on the right Pineapp[
Beauty.

2

Leaf Shapes and Colourings

Sporting – Pigmentation – Genetic factors

List of Botanical terms used.

Acuminate: long pointed.

Allele: one individual gene of several which might become located in a particular place on a chromosome.

Anastomose: (veins) enlarged and interconnected.

Attenuated: tapered or thinned down.

Cordate: heart-shaped.

Crenate: rounded segments.

Cultivar: (syn. variety) a uniform vegetative stock propagated vegetatively.

Cuneate: wedge-shaped.

Dentate: with a toothed edge or margin.

Laciniated: slashed or cut into narrow sections.

Linear: with parallel edges and at least four times as long as broad.

Ovate: oval, but wider at the base.

Reticulated: network.

Serrate: with pointed teeth projecting forwards.

Somatic: referring to the tissue of the plant and not to the germ cells

Truncate: ending abruptly as though cut off.

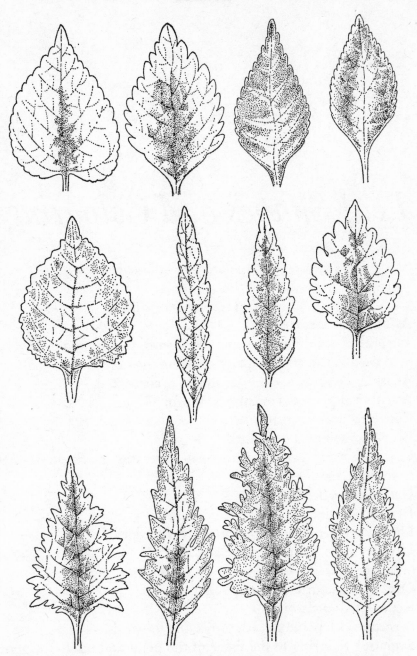

Example of some of the leaf shapes from the New Hybrids seed strain.

LEAF SHAPES AND COLOURING

It is certain that when most people envisage a coleus, the image coming to mind will be that of a plant bearing simple ovate leaves and possessing very few basic colour patterns. Indeed, some very popular and lovely seed strains have been developed for the purpose of providing plants of uniform colour and leaf form. These strains are valuable to gardeners when uniformity of colour and type are the chief requirements but unfortunately the greater part of coleus plants seen are of this description. The person cherishing the occasional potted coleus plant which has been grown from seed for home decoration is often unaware of those which have diverse forms and shapes of leaves, which, together with the great variety and complexity of colouring provide an endless source of pleasure. Let us recall the leaf forms of some of the original types.

The leaves of *C. blumei*, when introduced, were described as being rhomboidal ovate, with coarsely cut serrations, the end terminating in a long acuminate point. The base of the leaf, which was cuneate, was attenuated from the petiole. The veins were running almost parallel to the midrib. A specimen of this description is in the Kew herbarium with a signed note written in Sir Wm. Hooker's handwriting so we may expect this specimen to be typical of this period. *C. blumei* was followed by *C. pectinatus* (comb-like), and had deeply cut serrations.

C. verschaffeltii had a leaf base described as being either broadly cordate or truncated. That is, being more or less square across or even 'heart-ear'shaped. The edges were very wavy and undulated; the segments formed by the crenations were larger than in *C. blumei,* being egg-shaped and rounded (not pointed) and often toothed themselves. The texture of the leaf was velvety and soft and the purple pigmentation extended to the stems of the plant and was not confined to the leaves. (Indeed, exposed roots can often be seen pigmented where they are exposed to light.)

Wm. Bull offered a form of *C. aromaticus* described as having 'hairy green stems and leaves, the latter being flat, ovate in outline, crenated and of a fleshy texture . . . having a . . . thyme-like odour of a most agreeable character . . . possibly by fertilisation its fragrance may be imparted to the variegated series of this now popular family.' Mr. Bull introduced others from the Pacific with different leaf shapes and qualities.

C. veitchii and *C. gibsonii* were both introduced by Mr. John G. Veitch. They had large heart-shaped leaves with margins scarcely crenated. Many other coleus of lesser horticultural importance were introduced during the 19th century and we give details of these elsewhere. There is no doubt that some of these would be used, when compatible, for breeding, both in Europe and in their place of origin.

When studying herbarium specimens it is very noticeable that specimens described as *C. blumei* exhibit very wide variation in leaf form. One such at Kew has a digitated leaf, like a multi-fingered hand. Another is widely wedge-shaped like an extended fan, the leaf ending abruptly, truncated in a straight row of crenations. Also described as *C. blumei* are forms with long linear-shaped leaves, some resembling broad grass blades. Coleus closely resembling this latter form are described in present day horticulture as 'Croton-leaved' as they so closely resemble certain Codiaeum in shape. In Britain the winter leaf form of this type is often quite different from that produced in the summer time. During the darker, shorter days they grow much broader and often entirely green and do not assume their attractiveness until near to the spring equinox.

In the typical coleus leaf the principal veins stand out from the surface on the underside of the leaf, being, as it were, laid on to the surface and partially submerged. The network of lesser veins lies deeper in the leaf tissue, being entirely covered.

An interesting variation in leaf form is one affecting veination. The veins are not always uniformly arranged throughout the leaf blade as normally, but areas in which they are much thicker and reticulated occur in a systematic pattern forming an anas-

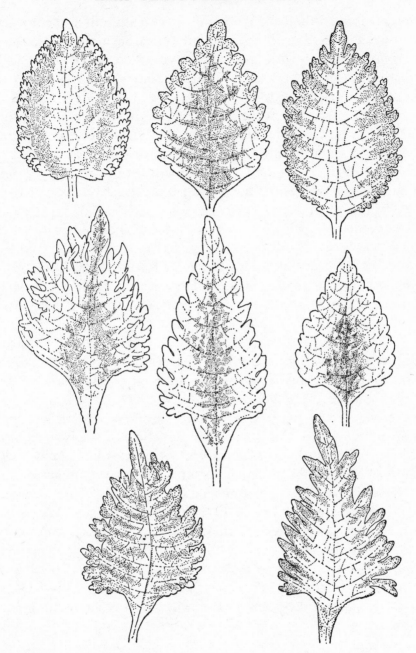

Some of the diverse shapes to be found amongst the Exhibition cultivars.

tomose area on the leaf. We noticed this feature first in cultivars of the ' Paisley Shawl ' group. Only once have we seen a herbarium specimen with this curious veination. This had a leaf identical in shape and size to ' Paisley Shawl ' and was collected at Beingin in the State of Malacca, growing in the fence of a garden in 1918. When this factor is passed on to plants of the Verschaffeltii type the anastomose area is often involved at the base of the segments, creating very beautiful leaf edges.

Some seed strains and certain named cultivars have large spreading leaves. These have a certain attractiveness and look impressive when young but such leaves soon sag downwards at their points, due to their weight, and, bending across their widest parts, easily crack and break. Large flat leaves seem also to show up collected dust more than the lesser leaved types. The loss of or damage to a single leaf on a large leaved plant is always a serious matter, but the loss of several leaves on a small leaved plant may not affect its appearance at all.

We have noticed that sometimes leaf margins roll upwards and inwards causing the upper surfaces of the leaf to become ' dished '. When this happens the most attractive surface, the upper one, becomes hidden and in consequence the general appearance of the plant is impaired. Curiously, odd leaves will sometimes sport to this feature, but sometimes a whole shoot or a whole plant will do so. This feature was noticed in 1939 by T. B. Post who noted the irregular manner in which it occurred and suggested that a particular genetic instability may be the cause.[1]

Many delightful kinds of Coleus have arisen as sports; more often than not certain families of cultivars sport, constantly producing the same sports. Often, sports can be anticipated. Sometimes there will be a slight variation on a leaf, possibly a small spot or larger area which is different. Usually this will occur again higher up the plant on the same side, becoming more pronounced as the growth progresses, ultimately emerging as a complete axillary shoot. Sometimes leaves appear with both halves quite different, divided by the mid rib. This often indicates that the axillary bud will be a sport. Occasionally a plant will become unstable, producing several sports at the same time. We have seen a plant bearing as many as six different shoots concurrently. It is not unusual for the writers to exchange comments about certain stock plants. 'Have you noticed " so-and-so " in No. 3 bay has produced that " such-and-such " type of sport again?' ' Yes, but it won't be any use, it's not an improvement.' A large proportion of sports that occur are undesirable, the leaf's visible features being rearranged in a less attractive manner.

A curious sporting occurs sometimes in the arrangement of the breaks. Coleus, being labiates, have four-sided stems and produce side branches in opposite pairs, alternating in progression of growth. Now and then a plant will be noticed which has a six sided main stem, the branches being arranged in whorls of three. The side breaks are, however, square in section and quite normal. This particular type of sporting does not continue throughout the plant's life. It is generally seen on young plants and appears to 'grow out' with maturity. On one occasion we saw an eight-sided main stem. A main stem will sometimes sport by developing a corkscrew twist, progressing a quarter turn at each node upwards as the plant develops. We have also seen flower spikes faciated.

The colouring of coleus leaves is caused by a combination of many factors. The study of these would involve a highly complex biochemical and genetic study far beyond the scope of a simple book such as this, but when growing these lovely plants to perfection it is helpful to have a grasp of certain of the basic functions taking place within the plant which are affecting its appearance and condition. First, let us briefly consider a number of the plant pigments involved.

The green colouring is of course created by chlorophyll. This is located in the grana of the chloroplasts of the cells. It is the vital pigment used by plants for utilising sunlight in the manufacture of carbohydrates. The pigment is being manufactured continually by a growing green plant to keep pace with the demands created by its increasing stature and also to replace that which becomes lost to it through destruction by light. To maintain itself in the normal healthy state in which chlorophyll can be generated freely, the plant needs an ample supply of those essential elements which it obtains in solution from the soil, plus carbon dioxide, sugar, sunlight and sufficient heat. Too much sunlight, however, will destroy chlorophyll and give the plant a shock sufficient to check its growth seriously. Evidence of this condition can often be seen after spells of sunny summer weather; coleus can become so badly bleached due to the loss of chlorophyll that several weeks of growing time may be needed to allow the plants to develop additional normal leaves before their lost beauty can be restored. Such a shock often causes older leaves to drop off prematurely.

When a coleus plant is growing strongly, particularly during that part of its development which may be termed its 'youth' and rapid growth is being made, green predominates as a contributory pigment to its appearance.

The pigments causing yellow hues belong to the carotenoids. There are many different pigments in this group covering yellow, orange, brown (and sometimes red) colours. The carotenoids consist of long carbon chains with carbon rings at each end. One sub-group, the carotenes, provide nature with many bright hues and makes attractive a wide range of leaves, fruits, flowers and animal products, e.g. peppers, rose hips, marigolds, apricots, pumpkins, carrots, butter, to name but a few. Carotenes can be extracted with chloroform, carbon disulphide or petroleum ether. Some are convertible into vitamin A. Carotenes are relatively stable in structure and are not easily decomposed when exposed to heat or strong sunlight; they are present in most chlorophyll-bearing leaves, the pigment usually being located along with the chlorophyll in the chloroplasts, but not always so.

As leaves become older and less vigorous (and consequently contain less chlorophyll than formerly) pigments which earlier had been masked by the abundance of chlorophyll become more dominant in colour and display themselves in hues and tones unimaginable. Certain coleus varieties which produce yellow and amber shades in the autumn are normally quite uniformly green

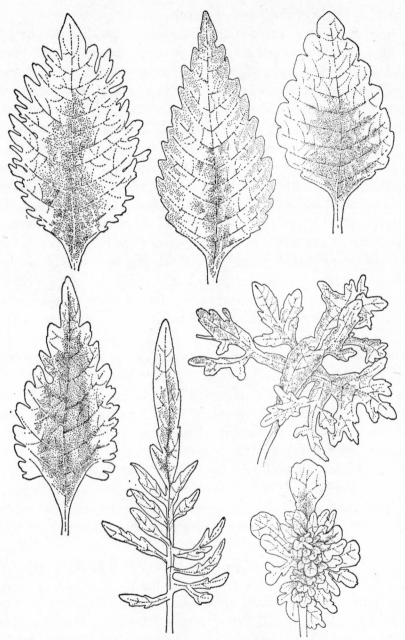

The three bottom right illustrations show how diverse are the leaf shapes to be found in Fantasia coleus. The others are Exhibition kinds.

throughout most of the summer months.

Another group of carotenoids is the carotenols (Xanthophylls). These are not hydrocarbons proper as they contain oxygen. They are insoluble in water, slightly soluble in petroleum ether and readily soluble in alcohol. Different pigments of this group are responsible for many of the yellows in nature, for instance dandelions, sunflowers, egg yolk and maize. The most common one of this group is Lutein, especially noticeable in autumn tints.

Yet another major group of plant pigment is the anthocyanins. These are responsible for most of the red, violet and blue colours. anthocyanins can be extracted with alcohol. They are not soluble in benzene or ether but are soluble in water (hence the strong red colour of the water in which beetroot has been boiled). The pigment is sometimes found as crystal, but it is nearly always distributed in solution throughout the cell cytoplasm. Anthocyanins belong to a chemical group known as glycosides, one feature of which is that of being able to produce a sugar when the molecule is broken down.

In 1921 Schertz[2] noted that leaves of coleus were very prone to loss of chlorophyll and that the addition of nitrogen to the soil kept them green. He also reported that the carotin and xanthophyll content greatly increased as the leaves mottled with age. We must remember this point when we are tempted to be over-generous with nitrogen. Coleus will not grow with bright colours if they are over-dosed and kept green with nitrogenous plant growth stimulants. It is certain that other pigments will be present and play some minor part in the colouring of these lovely plants but it is from among the foregoing that the principal ones are to be found.

Pigmentation may be intense, slight or absent in any particular area. The coloration may be on one surface of the leaf blade only, or on both surfaces, or it may be blotched, streaked or spotted on both surfaces. When areas of the same colour coincide on both surfaces of a leaf, a strong shade is created. When different colours are blotched on both leaf surfaces they create a fascinating array of different hues as they interpose and overlie each other. Differing amounts of red, yellow and green provide an almost limitless spectrum. Dark green and red creates brown; pale green and red creates scarlet etc. Some plants are all one uniform shade throughout, being beautifully plain and peerless, lemon yellow, warm bronze and even almost black. Some have leaves with pure white centres; some with highly coloured stems. Others have their colour patterns linked with their veination or their leaf margins. Some look like choice lacework. Certain ones have faintly pubescent leaves which, when in good condition, are attractively bloomed in texture like a grape.

We have mentioned the effects that environment (temperature, light, nutrition) can have upon the plant's appearance, but of course the factors governing the distribution of pigmentation and the arrangement of leaf form are genetic. Environment can certainly make a lot of difference to the plant's appearance but that upon which environment exerts an influence is genetic in origin.

An interesting résumé by D. C. Rife upon the genetics of coleus was published in 1948.[3] A considerable amount of research was reported from which it was established that thirteen sets of alleles were responsible for leaf colour and shape. From the nine alleles mentioned as being responsible for leaf colour, 137,781 different genotypes were theoretically possible by breeding. In practice some of the more beautiful traits are recessive and it is only by using certain breeding techniques that these traits appear freely amongst progeny.

D. C. Rife pointed out that when the alleles governing the shallow lobing of leaves interacted with the alleles affecting the deep lobes, a very curious and much divided leaf could result. (Fig. 11 D.)

We noticed this occurring in our crosses in 1959, several years before D. C. Rife's paper came to our notice. The first young plants were quite green, resembling curious antlers and with very little leaf blade attached.

Since 1959 it has been possible to create types of some of these new forms, breeding into them strong colours and even multicolours. A selection of these was first introduced to public dis-

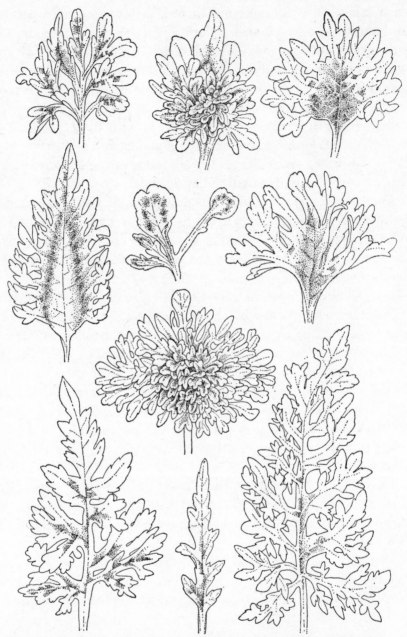

This plate shows the fascinating diversity of Fantasia leaf shapes, from the simple fingered form (upper centre) to the elaborate involved tufted form (lower centre).

play by the writers at Southport Flower Show in August 1972.

This completely different form of *Coleus blumei* became known as 'Fantasia' Coleus. Some forms resemble in shape the leaves of a woodland fern, others are similar to curly kale or parsley; some have leaf edges tasselled and frilled with numerous leaf-like segments, each one being separately frilled itself. A few kinds are like posies, almost resembling a small bouquet of gaily coloured leaves.

On some plants which have frilled leaves it will be seen that this tendency also involves the flowers also. In addition to the corolla sections being extra parted the reproductive organs are often deformed, causing the flower to be sterile.

1   *Journal of Heredity.* 30. 27-31. 1939. T. B. Post. Ruffled Coleus
2   *Botanical Gazette* 71. 127-128. 1921. Schertz. *A Chemical and Physio-logical Study of Mottling of Leaves*
3   *Journal of Heredity.* 39. 85-91. 1948. D. C. Rife. *Simply inherited variations of Coleus*

3

Botany

The Classification of Coleus and Plectranthus
C. laciniatus benth
C. scutellarioides benth
C. pumilus blanco

Tuberous forms of Plectranthus and Coleus
C. thyrsoideus
C. frederici
C. shirensis
C. aromaticus
C. amboinicus
P. fruticosus
P. behrii
P. oertendahlii
P. coleoides
P. hirtus benth

In our foreword we expressed our intention of writing to provide general information for the average amateur gardener rather than to compile a text book for the few. This object is a difficult one to fulfil when dealing with the botany of these plants. Although it would be academically desirable for botanical data to be related in full in the traditional style, this would, we believe, be tedious and heavy for most readers and as generalisations cannot be made about detail of this kind without the risk of misleading ambiguity, we are striking a balance between the two and suggest to those who wish to look deeper that they might follow up the references given for precise detail. The situation is not a straightforward one, as will be seen.

Let us recall L. H. Bailey's comments about *Coleus blumei*. 'This species, founded on cultivated plants in Java is probably to be regarded as now understood an assemblage or combination of species.' The more significant words in this phrase are ' cultivated plants' and ' assemblage or combination '. In other words, *Coleus blumei bentham* as we know it has evolved at the hands of man. Once, we heard it described as a 'Super Mongrel' and this remark sums it up aptly.

We often wondered precisely how many basic species of ornamental Coleus there really were (if it ever could be really established beyond doubt) and how many so-called species might really be different populations which have been brought into being as a result of the geography of the area in which they were found; the South West Pacific, containing multitudes of land areas separated by sea, would contribute towards the likelihood of this occurring.

In our early breeding work we soon noticed that many different features of leaf, habit and flower formation appeared and reappeared in different assemblages with successive generations. It became our usual procedure to establish almost any particular feature that appeared desirable into a type by simple line breeding. Provided that such a type was then prevented from being crossed with another one it would become progressively more uniform with each succeeding year. Nevertheless, it is true to say that coleus exhibit a degree of variation from the standard much greater than most plants. This is so even with strains of seed acknowledged as ' fixed '. Somatic mutation also occurs at a very high rate, especially in certain groupings of related cultivars.

There is no doubt that earlier botanists had difficulty in placing some of these plants. More recent floras contain many synonyms and collective re-groupings of earlier species under fewer headings. Botanists point out that various species interbreed and pass into one another in many instances.

The genus Coleus is, as we pointed out in Chapter 1, very closely allied to Plectranthus. Originally, both were classed in the genus Ocimum, but the botanist Linnaeus, who reformed the system of classifying plants according to their reproductive organs maintained that the most important feature of Ocimum was the toothed stamen filaments. Later L'Heritier (1784) placed those species which had no such tooth into a separate genus which he named plectranthus, (πληΚτρον, a cock's spur and ανθοs a flower) such a spur being on the upper side of the base of the corolla of some species. This latter feature was reiterated by Lamarck four years later.

It was Loureiro who separated off and named the genus Coleus (1790). He placed those species which had their stamens fused together and united into a tube into this new genus. The word coleus comes from Κολεοs, meaning sheath, which the stamens form as they are united at their base, as opposed to plectranthus in which (it was supposed) they were free.

Botanical Magazine, 1812, No. 1446, published an article on *Ocimum scutellarioides* (*Coleus scutellarioides*). Some of the accompanying remarks give ample evidence of the flux of botanical opinion of the day. It reads '. . . Linnaeus in his *Mantissa Prima*, observed that this species differed so much in the form of the flower from the rest, as almost to render it a distinct genus; and Professor Vahl since added Ocimum zatarhendi of Forskohl, an undoubted congener of our plant, to plectranthus: Willdenow, having adopted this change, ought also to have placed this under the same genus, as has been done by R. Brown, in his *Prodromus Florae Novae Hollandiae*. But as this author has remarked that the genus Ocimum requires altogether to undergo a re-examination, both to decide which of the species have processes to their filaments, and of what value this, as yet dubious, character is in determining the genus; and especially as he has not removed

The New Hybrids Orange brown specimen

Paisley Shawl. Its green leaf centre, speckled brown, and
cream border, speckled red, make it quite distinct from
any other variety.

The New Hybrids. An arrangement of four self-colours
taken from the general mixture of plants.

The New Hybrids Red specimen

Winter Sun. A first-class exhibition sort from cuttings only.

The New Hybrids Red specimen

this plant in the new edition of the *Hortus Kewensis*, we have thought it best to leave it under Ocimum; especially as it is very doubtful whether the ecalcarati or those species which have no such spur, of which this is one, may not, in the general reform, be again separated from the plectranthus L'Heritier.'

Blume did not use the fusion of the stamens as a distinguishing feature in his *Bijdragen tot de Flora Nederlandsch Indie* 1826. Bentham, however, did use this in his *Genera and Species Labiatae* 1832. On p. 47 he gave the following reasons for his adopting this change. 'The monadelphous stamina, which distinguish these plants from all others of this tribe, and even of the order of Labiatae, have been frequently observed; and although made use of by Loureiro to characterise the genus, have not, as already mentioned, been considered by Brown and others of sufficient importance to separate Coleus from Plectranthus; but as, among the number of species now known, they all, with the exception of *C. scutellarioides*, and two or three others only, are so distinct in habit as to be recognised without examination of the stamina; and as these two or three also differ from Plectranthus by the truncate lateral lobes of the calyx, and have always a tendency to the cymiform inflorescence, I have thought it advisable to adopt Loureiro's genus. At the same time it must be admitted that the under-mentioned sections are as different from one another in habit as that of Solenostemon is from Coleoides, a section of Plectranthus, and might almost be considered as so many distinct genera, were not the form of the corolla (always much influenced by the stamina) so nearly the same in all.'

Other botanists have created new genera for re-classifying sections of the coleus-plectranthus complex according to various other details of their flower structure: e.g. the shape of the corolla tube, the shape and form of the calyx teeth and the fusion of pairs of stamens. Nevertheless it would appear that no basic simple system for classifying coleus, which is acceptable to all, has yet been devised.

In 1962 J. K. Morton examined the situation of the classifications of coleus and plectranthus in the *Journal of the Linnaean*

Society. After reviewing the history of this complex he stated
' That the fusion or otherwise of the stamens does not form a
satisfactory basis for separating Coleus from Plectranthus is
manifestly obvious from an examination of the now large amount
of West African material. The use of this character is in my
opinion entirely arbitrary and has led to the separation of closely
allied taxa. In some species it appears that the degree of fusion
is sufficiently variable for different populations of the same species
to be placed in different genera. . . . One cannot help but be
struck by the many similar cases in which species have been
described under both Coleus and Plectranthus, or have been
transferred from one genus to the other, by different workers
using the same criterion of staminal fusion in distinguishing these
genera.

' As the stamens do not form a basis for separating these two
genera, we are left with the alternatives of finding another more
satisfactory character or of combining the two genera. I have
been unable to do the former and am therefore obliged to follow
Brown and Blume in combining the two genera under the prior
name of Plectranthus.' He later discussed the possibility of
chromosome counts as a criterion for limiting the genera. Unfortunately, this method bore no more likely chance of success because different base numbers were not at all uncommon and the
occurrence of cytotypes in certain species suggested that chromosome number is not very stable and may alter by the multiplica-
tion or loss of individual chromosomes. If then, we are to accept
J. K. Morton's qualified exposition we should really call our
beautiful coloured Coleus Plectranthus L'Herit.

A colloquial botanical description of the cultivated Coleus
Blumei might read as follows:

Class	*Didynamia*
Natural order	*Labiatae*
Genus	*Coleus loureiro*
Species	*blumei*

General character. Annual herb or shrubby perennial. *Height.* 30 cms. to 3 metres or more. *Stems* and branches square, often coloured, angles generally obtuse, the joints often hairy. *Leaves* rhomboid ovate, deltoid ovate, linear to lanceolate, $\frac{1}{2}$ cm. to 25 cms. wide by 1 cm. to 30 cms. long. Their edges incisio or serrate; sometimes digitately lobed; sometimes entire. Apex acuminate or acute. Membranaceous, pubescent or sub-glabrous on both surfaces, attenuated into the petiole or cordate; becoming smaller and cuspidate ascending upper flowering stems. *Petioles* usually pubescent at the sides $\frac{1}{2}$ cm. to 8 cms. long. *Leaf-blade* green or yellow green, frequently blotched, spotted or striate with purple, brown, pink, red, white or self-coloured. Often uniform purple beneath. Principal nerves partially raised on underside only. *Inflorescence* terminal whorled racemes, panicles or cymes, sometimes branched, 10 cms. to 60 cms. in height, bractated, shedding after pollination. *Calyx* 2 mm. to 3 mm. long, oval, broader at the base, bell-shaped, bearing fruit, declining downwards, usually very pubescent outside but glabrous inside; upper lobe entire, oval with edges turning downwards; lower lip three parted, the middle lobe being itself parted into two triangular pointed teeth protruding beyond the upper; the side lobes shorter and oval-ended, closing inwards and retaining nutlets after pollination as calyx enlarges. *Corolla* violet or very occasionally bluish white, funnel-shaped, protruding downwards, curved, or more often than not sharply bent and refracted, 4 mm. to 6 mm. long. Corolla limb double lipped, the upper lip short and broad, erect, three cleft; the lower one extended, boat-shaped, bearing the stamens and style. *Stamens* four, united into a tube for more than half their length and encompassing the style. *Style* protruding beyond the anthers and bearing a bifid stigma. Nutlets four in number, black or dark brown flattened spheres, about 1 mm. in diameter.

Botanical references: *Coleus Blumei Benth. Genera & Species Labiatae* p. 56; *De Candolle, Prodromus Systematis Naturalis,* XII p. 75; *Botanical Magazine* 4754 (1853); *Records of the Botanical Survey of India* (1940) vol. 14, no. 1, p. 55.

Coleus laciniatus Benth. Although this species is not generally found in commerce as such, its botanical features can often be seen amongst named cultivars and hybrids purporting to be Blumei. The species is identified by its having deeply and irregularly cut and incised leaves. The leaf base is characteristically wedge-shaped from the petiole. The calyx is densely hairy outside. In 1946 D. C. Rife and H. C. Duber in their report *Genes and Species Differences in Coleus* questioned whether *C. laciniatus* could be regarded as a species distinct from Blumei. Their research established that the irregularity of leaves was due to a single pair of genes only and in all other respects the species were identical. It is native to Malaya and adjacent islands. Genera & Species Labiatae p. 56. *Records of the Botanical Survey of India* (1940) vol. 14, no. 1, p. 56.

Coleus scutellarioides Bentham. This Coleus was mentioned by Rumphius as Majana Rubra. *Botanical Magazine* (1812) No. 1446 reported it as Ocimum Scutellarioides. In 1862 Florre des Serres informed its readers that forms of it were cultivated in gardens in India and the South West Pacific Islands. Different forms were introduced into Europe and given names. It is really a native of Australia and Malaya. In general, the plant's habit is more erect than typical Blumei.

The leaves are ovate lanceolate, usually crenated. Both leaf surfaces and the calyx are free of hair; the underside of the leaf is gland spotted, also the calyx. The leaves are variable but usually very dark purple in colour, sometimes almost black. Merrill in his translation of *Rumphius Herbarium Amboinense*, p. 460, makes the following observation, ' Majana rubra Rumph. was originally and erroneously reduced by Linnaeus to Ocimum frutescens Linn., in Stickman Herb. Amb. (1754) 22, Amoen. Acad. 4 (1759) 131, Syst. ed. 10 (1759) 1105. Recognising this error, however, Linnaeus, Sp. Pl. ed. 2 (1763) 834, made the Rumphian description and figure the whole basis of Ocimum scutellarioides Linn., which in turn is the basis of Coleus scutellarioides Benth. Burman f., Fl. Ind. (1768) 129, erroneously referred it to Ocimum gratissimum Linn.'

Rumphius. Herbarium Amboinense 5. 291, t. 101 (1747) Merrill translation p. 460; *Wallich Plantae Asiaticae Rariores* II p. 16; *Botanical Magazine* 1446 (1812); Bentham. *Genera & Species Labiatae* p. 53; Haines, *Botany of Bihar and Orisa*, p. 736; *Records of the Botanical Survey of India* (1940) vol. 14, no. 1, p. 54.

Coleus pumilus blanco. See earlier chapter for description, page 25. *Blanco Flora Filippines* (1837) p. 482; *Botanical Magazine* (1924) 9034; *Gartenflora* lxxv (1926) p. 360 (Coleus Rehneltianus Berger) *Revue Horticole* (1928) p. 180. (Coleus Rehneltianus Berger).

Numerous other types of ornamental Coleus have appeared in commerce from time to time but they have not become established by popular accord; they are to be seen in the books.

Seven forms of Plectranthus and Coleus bearing tubers, some being valuable as food, were described by Bois in 1901 in the *Bulletin de la Societe Botanique de France*, p. 107. His article was principally about *C. coppini,* cultivated in the Southern Sudan and in Nigeria. The edible tubers were produced at the base of the plant and also at the nodes; these were blackish brown in colour with white flesh. They attained a size of about 55 mm. in length by approximately 25 mm. in diameter. The natives called this crop ' Ousounifing ' which literally means ' small black potato '.

In addition to *C. coppini*, the following six forms were listed. The references in brackets have been added by ourselves.

1. Plectranthus ternatus Sims. Widely grown in Equatorial Africa and known in the Transvaal as ' Matambala '. (*Botanical Magazine* 2460, 1824)

2. Plectranthus esculentus, N. E. Brown, of Natal. (Hooker, *Icones Plantarum*, xxv. 2488. 1896)

3. Plectranthus floribundus N. E. Brown, of tropical Africa. This has yellow flowers and is known as the ' Kaffir Potato '. (Hooker, *Icones Plantarum* xxv. 2489. 1896)

4. Coleus tuberosus Benth. This is grown as a food crop in Ceylon, South East Asia and the East Indies. (*Genera & Species Labiatae*. p. 59)

5. *Coleus edulis Vatke*, grown in Abyssinia, often at a height of six or seven thousand feet in altitude.

6. *Coleus Barbatus Benth*, grown in India, Arabia and the tropical east coast of Africa. (*Records of the Botanical Survey of India* (1940) vol. 14, no. 1, p. 53, under *C. forskohlii.*)

(In connection with the foregoing see also Coleus Parviflorus Bentham in *Records of the Botanical Survey of India* (1940), vol. 14, no. 1, p. 54, and Backer, *Flora of Java* (1965) II, p. 637.)

G. Taylor, commenting upon *C. esculentus* in *Journal of Botany*, LXIX, suppl. II, (1931), p. 159, comments ' The Angolan specimens in association with the other Tropical and South African material show that this widespread and often cultivated species is subject to very considerable variation. No fixed character can be found to distinguish the several species and varieties which have been proposed by earlier authors '.

A number of forms of Coleus and Plectranthus have been introduced into Europe as flowering plants. Most of these have originated in Africa. Many of the African species are outstanding for their beautiful blue flower spikes The most notable of these is *C. thyrsoideus*. The first cultivated plants were raised at Kew from seeds taken from herbarium specimens sent by Mr. A. Whyte. These were sown in April 1897 and the resulting plants flowered under heated glass in February of the following year, producing an abundance of beautiful bright gentian blue racemes, three inches wide and six to ten inches long.

The plant's introduction was acclaimed as an event of horticultural importance. *The Gardeners Chronicle* of February 11th 1899 stated, ' I know no other plant that is more effective in winter; certainly no plant at Kew has been more admired.' The plant was subsequently awarded the R.H.S. Award of Merit on December 18th 1900.

C. thyrsoideus grows on the plateau at the north eastern tip of Lake Nyasa. It also grows in Mozambique, and in Tanganyika at altitudes of about six to seven thousand feet.

In cultivation it is a quick-growing robust plant. Young plants may be reared from either seed or rooted cuttings in the same manner and style as *C. blumei*. To produce reasonably proportioned specimens it is advisable not to strike cuttings before late May or June. In general, this Coleus is better when grown slightly cooler than blumei, keeping the night temperature down to about 50°F. We have heard of small, attractive pots of this plant being raised by striking six or eight shoots together in a $4\frac{1}{2}''$ pot, using as cuttings the flower shoots themselves, striking them as soon as it is obvious that the flowers have formed. The plants require good ventilation and shade during hot, bright weather to prevent leaf scorch.

Botanical Magazine 7672 (1899).
Gardeners' Chronicle. Ser. III; xxix 39 (1901).
Journal Royal Horticultural Society 25, lxi.

Coleus fredericii is a beautiful blue-flowering perfumed Coleus flowering in the winter. A native of Angola, it was collected by Dr. Friedrich Welwitsch in 1857 and was classed in the genus Neomullera by Briquet. In 1931 G. Taylor pointed out that it ought really to have been placed in the genus Coleus. The plant enjoyed a spell of popularity at about this time but it is rarely seen at the present time. It usually grows to a height of 1 to $1\frac{1}{2}$ metres and bears large, ovate, pale-green leaves covered with fine bristle-like hairs on both surfaces.
Journal of Botany LXIX, suppl. II, 159 (1931).
Botanical Magazine 9421 (1935).

Yet another blue-flowering African species raised at Kew is *Coleus shirensis*. Seed of this plant was gathered in Zomba by Mr. J. McClounie in 1902. It grows to a height of about one metre with each branch terminating in a panicle of dark blue flowers in late winter. This is a very beautiful flowering plant. Being closely allied to *C. thyrsoideus* it requires the same treatment.
Botanical Magazine 8024 (1905).
Thistleton-Dyer. *Flora of Tropical Africa,* vol. 5, p. 443.

Coleus aromaticus, which was offered by William Bull during the 1870s is another type which is unfortunately unobtainable commercially in Europe at present. Mr. Bull described the form which he offered as ' An interesting stove plant, with hairy green stems and leaves, the latter being flat, ovate in outline, crenated and of a fleshy texture, and moreover remarkable for having a strong aromatic thyme-like odour of a most agreeable character. It is a native of India, and bears pale blue flowers. . . .'

Botanical Register XVIII 1832, quoted the botanist Bentham and reads, ' This plant appears to be very commonly cultivated in Indian gardens, chiefly on account of its great fragrance. The leaves are frequently eaten with bread and butter, or bruised and mixed with various articles of food, drink or medicine. It is probably also indigenous in that country; but in all the East Indian collections which I have seen, the specimens are taken from gardens, unless those marked as gathered at Patna in Hamilton's Herbarium be really wild. Roxburgh, in his MS Flora, . . .speaks of this plant as common in almost every garden where, however, it seldom flowers.' Bailey, in *Hortus Second* (1941) writes, ' Shoots sometimes seen in markets as " Spanish Thyme ".' This plant is reported to be valuable in the treatment of cholera (Chatergee and others).

Bentham Genera & Species Labiatae, p. 51.
De Candolle, *Prodromus Systematis Nat. XII* p. 72;
Wallich, *Plantae Asiaticae Rariores*, II, p. 16.
Botanical Register XVIII (1832), t. 1520.
Records of the Botanical Survey of India (1940) vol. 14, no. 1, p. 54.
Science and Culture (Chatergee and others) vol. 24, (1958) p. 241-3.
Coleus aromaticus is now classed under *C. amboinicus* Lour.

Coleus amboinicus Lour. E. D. Merrill in *Transactions of American Philosophical Society* (1935), part II, p. 343, comments, ' The species, one with fleshy, very aromatic leaves, is widely cultivated in the Indo-Malaysian region. *Marrubium album amboinicum* Rumph. (Herb. Amb. 5:294. pl. 102. f2) cited by Louriero as a synonym, and whence he took his specific name, is correctly placed. In habit and general appearance this species is remarkably distinct from other species of Coleus.' The plant is best described as a fleshy shrub with fleshy, broadly ovate leaves, crenate, with rounded bases.

Flora Cochinchinensis 372. (1790)

Backer, *Flora of Java II* (1965), p.637.

Records of the Botanical Survey of India (1940) vol. 14, no. 1, p. 54.

A number of Plectranthus sufficiently attractive as ornamental plants have from time to time appeared upon the horticultural scene. Several of these have become popular as greenhouse and house-plants; others are occasionally seen in specialists' collections or Parks' Department conservatories. The following are of interest.

Plectranthus fruticosus L'Herit. According to Aiton in *Hortus Kewensis* II, p.322 (1789), this plant was introduced from the Cape of Good Hope by Mr. F. Masson in 1774. It was illustrated in L'Heritier's *Stirpes novae aut minus cognitae*, t.41 (1786).

This plant, as stated earlier, is very robust and will thrive in a cool frost-free situation, attaining a height of about 2 metres if permitted. Its stems are four-sided and bear short bristly hairs. The habit is erect and branching. The leaves are green, opposite, mostly broadly ovate, coarsely serrate dentate. The upper surface is sparsely covered with short brownish-gold hairs; the veins underneath are covered more densely so. Both surfaces are dotted with minute yellow glands. The flowers generally form branching pyramids of up to 25 cms. high made up, usually, of triplets of sessile flowers, sometimes bractated. The calyx is gland dotted and covered with short hairs. The blue corolla tube is straight, about 8 mm. long and bears a conspicuous spur standing erect near the base of the tube on its upper side. The upper lip of the corolla is heart-shaped, standing erect resembling two 'wings'. It is also attractively spotted with dark markings. The under lip is egg-shaped, and being attached at its smaller end bends downwards and backwards underneath the corolla tube, exposing the four stamens and the pistil projecting forwards.

Propagation is by cuttings inserted in the usual manner in early spring and later potted into a good rich potting compost.

Provide good growing conditions with moderate light and water to keep the plant short jointed. It is, as its name implies, a bushy plant by nature.

This plant has been misdescribed in the past. *Nicholson's Dictionary* shows a plant with flowers obviously not *P. fruticosus*. Marloth's *Flora of South Africa*, III, part 2, plate 46, fig. 3, also shows a flower which is not to type. According to Burtt in *Botanical Magazine* 9616 (1940-42), the plant shown is a form of *Plectranthus ecklonii Benth*. At the time of writing, a variegated form of *P. hirtus Benth*. is circulating in Britain wrongly described as *P. fruticosus*.

Bentham Genera & Species Labiatae 32 (1832).
De Candolle, *Prodromus Systematis Naturalis XII* 62 (1848).
Gartenflora XIII 98, t. 431 (1864).
Bailey *Standard Cyclopaedia Hort*. V 2712 (1916).
Botanical Magazine 9616.

Plectranthus örtendahlii. This delightful plant is well-known as a house and greenhouse plant on account of its attractive leaves and pretty flowers. Its trailing, creeping habit makes it an excellent subject for interior hanging baskets and troughs or as individual pot plants. The leaves are thick and fleshy, broad, up to 8 cms. across, pale green, the margins slightly crenate. The veination is white. The leaf edges are purple blushed, as are their undersides when old.

The flowers are carried in whorls on spikes of about 15 cms. to 20 cms. high, sometimes branched. The corolla tube is curiously inflated at the base, narrowing to the lips. The upper lips are winged, erect; the lower one declining downwards. The stamens and style are exposed forwards. The colour of the corolla is a curious pastel shade of off-white with a suggestion of delicate lilac-pink. It flowers in the late autumn.

Propagation is best done by taking fresh cuttings each early spring. Like Coleus they root readily in a striking mixture. Potting several together in a 10 cm. pot provides a sizeable plant quickly. Keep well-watered, especially if used as a hanging plant. Shade from direct sunlight. Second year plants are not always successful, even when re-potted, and it is more practical to propagate new plants annually.

There is some doubt about the origin of this plant. Apparently it was noticed growing in the Botanical Gardens at Gothoburg. It had earlier been received by the Botanical Garden in Lund from Copenhagen bearing the name Plectranthus Saccatus Benth. It was subsequently established by Thore C. E. Fries that the plant was a new species. It was named after the academy lecturer at Upsala, I. Ortendahl.

Acta Hort. Gothoburgensis I (1924), 253.
Journal Royal Horticultural Society, 79. 266.
Journal Royal Horticultural Society, 83. 3.
A. B. Graff, Exotica 3. (1963) p. 1693. t. 1022.

Plectranthus behrii Compton. This beautifully flowered South African Plectranthus comes from Pondoland. It is a branching, upright woody shrub which attains a height of between $\frac{1}{2}$ to 1 metre or thereabouts. It is closely allied to *Plectranthus fruticosus.* The leaves are broad-ovate with an acute tip, green above and purple below; their margins crenate-dentate. The flowers are arranged on a terminal raceme of about 25 cms. long with lateral ones shorter. The corolla tube is a bright attractive mauve-pink, 6 to 8 mm. long. The upper lip is erect and 'winged', up to about 8 mm. wide, and spotted with deep pink spots. The lower lip is erect when young but is deflexed when full grown. The stamens are exserted, tilted upwards at first but rolling under and backwards later, the style remaining exserted with twin awl-shaped stigmas. The corolla tube carries a nectary spur similar to P. fruticosus on its upper side near the base of the tube. The calyx lobes are also pink.

This plant is a first-class autumn-flowering plant for the temperate greenhouse in Britain, flowering continuously for many weeks. *The Journal of South African Botany* II (1945) p. 124 states that 'It is an attractive and useful garden plant, flowering copiously and over a long period in late summer and being satisfactory in full sun or in partial shade.

It is easily raised from cuttings inserted in early spring. As its growth is inclined to be thin and wiry it needs stopping frequently during its early months to prevent the growth from becoming too open.

The writers crossed *P. Behrii* with *P. örtendahlii* in the fall of 1969 using the latter as seed parent. Our object was to produce a plant with shorter habit. The progeny resulting from this cross flowered in the autumn of 1970. Most carried foliage, flowers and stems like Behrii; one had a low bushy habit. This specimen produced flowers equal to the parent.

See also, *Flowering Plants of South Africa* (1951) t.1109.

Plectranthus coleoides. This plant was introduced into Britain in 1862 from the Nilghiri Mountains of Southern India. The native form produces a shrubby dwarf plant of between 30 cms. – 60 cms. in height bearing lurid green orbicular cordate crenated leaves. The stems are splashed with purple. The flowers of a purple colour are produced in late winter and early spring.

Botanical Magazine 5841 (1870).

Records of the Botanical Survey of India (1940) vol. 14, no. 1, p.48.

Fyson, *Flora of S. Indian Hill Stations II*, 404 (1932).

A form known as coleoides ' Marginatus ' has green deltoid ovate multi-crenate leaves, 5 to 8 cms. across. The edges are silver-white. The leaf blade is mottled and splashed with pale green and silver-grey. This plant is very attractive and showy for the greenhouse and conservatory. It requires culture comparable with coleus. It is tender and will shed its leaves upon suffering the slightest shock. Nevertheless it is very well worth cultivating.

Plectranthus hirtus Benth. variegatus. A variegated form of this South African plant is currently circulating in Britain amongst horticulturists. The growth is trailing and wiry often with the nodes 5 to 10 cms. apart. The individual growths often attain $1\frac{1}{2}$ to 3 metres or more in one season. The leaves are tiny, $1\frac{1}{2}$ to 3 cms. across, and ovate, crenate, with a cuneate base. The leaf margins are creamy white. The whole plant is strongly and delightfully aromatic.

The habit of this plant makes it first-class for use as an indoor trailing plant or outdoors in summer where it is not too exposed. The stems become hard and woody with one season's growth, subsequent growth generating at the nodes. Hanging baskets planted entirely with this Plectranthus are capable of producing solid vertical columns six or eight feet high in two or three years time. Small potted specimens can be obtained quickly during spring and early summer by striking several cuttings in a suitably sized pot. Its temperature range is between 50°F in winter to 75°F in summer. Shading from the full summer sun is required when grown under glass.

An inverse variegated form is also in existence; this has the silver markings admixed with green. The leaf edges are green. This form, too, is very attractive.

Plectranthus hirtus Bentham. Genera and Species Labiatae 1832. p. 38.

The following species are sometimes seen but they are of minor horticultural significance:

Coleus penzigii. An Abyssinian species covered with white downy hairs.

Plectranthus australis. A creeping herb, useful for trailing situations. $2\frac{1}{2}$ inch green, fleshy, almost circular leaves, crenate. Native to Australia and adjacent islands.

4

Coleus Culture

Climatology
Composts for
    (a)   potting-on
    (b)   seed sowing
    (c)   striking cuttings
Raising plants from seed
Raising plants from cuttings
Potting-on and after-care
Stopping
Flower spikes
Leaf-dropping and auxins
Ethylene

CLIMATE

The first essential to be considered before starting to grow Coleus is the climate needed by the plants. Like all other plants, they have evolved in a particular climate and if success in growing them is to be attained, they must be provided with a similar one or they will not thrive.

As they are native to particular tropical and sub-tropical parts

58

of the world their basic natural climatic requirements are satisfied with a temperature range of between 60°F (16°C), minimum winter, and 75°F (24°C), maximum in summer, good light, but not burning hot sun, and plenty of water. The mean temperature for Batavia in Java, from which country *Coleus blumei* was introduced, is 80°F (27°C) for the whole year with a daily average divergence of not more than 13°F (7°C) throughout. These conditions are easily obtained in an unheated glasshouse from mid May onwards up to the autumn, the season being extended in the South.

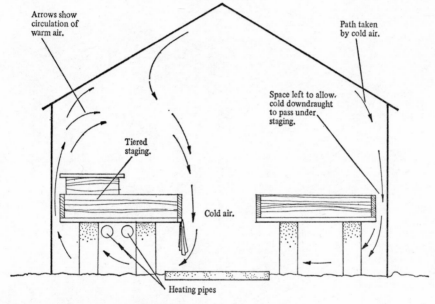

Arrows show circulation of warm air.

Path taken by cold air.

Space left to allow cold downdraught to pass under staging.

Tiered staging.

Cold air.

Heating pipes

Layout of the Greenhouse
If the heating installation is under a side bench it is beneficial to attach a polythene curtain along the front of the bench. The curtain should be hung to within a few inches of the ground. The curtain prevents the heat from escaping at the front of the bench and causes it to rise behind the bench as shown by the arrows. This convected heat puts a blanket of warmer air over the plants and deflects colder air towards the centre path. The tiered staging shown in the diagram may be supported on concrete blocks.

In practice Coleus, when established, can tolerate occasional drops in temperature as low as 50°F (10°C) but unless extreme care is taken over their watering, losses will occur. At temperatures lower than 50°F (10°C) it is not reasonable to expect success as the life force and vigour of the plants will be at such a low ebb that they are unable to resist rotting organisms, particularly of the roots, and to a lesser degree of the stems also. At higher temperatures this hazard does not occur as the plants can adequately resist them. An adequate temperature range for growing Coleus throughout the four seasons is between 60°F (16°C) and 70°F (24°C); a temperature higher than this, though acceptable, is quite unnecessary for success.

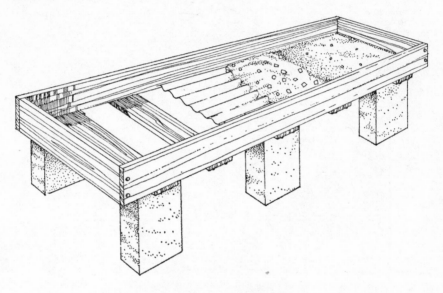

An easily made staging or bench for growing Coleus
The sides and ends of the staging are made from five or six-inch floorboards. Three-inch wide batons are nailed across from one side to the other on the base of the box-like structure and these batons support sheets of corrugated asbestos which can then be covered with a suitable aggregate. Since you will be using a watering can, it is best to use three-inch galvanised nails for fastening. The timber may be second-hand and should be painted after assembly with Green Wood Preserver. The illustration shown is of a bench with a working surface about twenty two inches above ground level, additional height may be gained by supporting the concrete blocks on brick bases. This type of glasshouse bench may be constructed to any length and is easily converted to a Capillary-Action Sand Bench.

The New Hybrids Frilled, deep red

A closer look at the simple but effective pattern and colours of Winter Sun.

The New Hybrids Frilled, red specimen

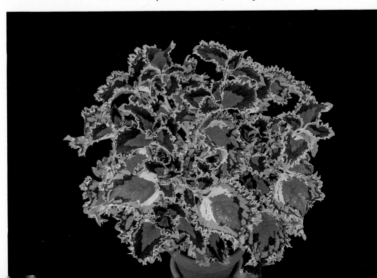

A hanging basket of coleus. The narrow-leaved, slender croton varieties lend themselves very effectively to this type of display. Red Croton around the outside with Buttermilk in the centre.

Pineapple Beauty, being trained as a standard. Thi lends itself very well to this purpose.

Walter Turner. A leading exhibition sort which makes a bushy plant more easily than most.

The provision of shade and of adequate watering are climatic considerations which will be dealt with under ' Culture '. Critical attention must be paid to both these points. In this connection we must remember that the ornamental Coleus's natural home had skies which for most of the year became increasingly cloudy each day as the sun climbed higher in the sky, with rain falling in the afternoons.

COMPOSTS

In common with most other plants of a similar nature, Coleus benefit from the use of different composts at different times, each one catering for the specific needs of the plant at that particular time; these are seed-sowing, cutting-striking, summer-growing in pots and occasionally over-wintering.

We will discuss potting compost first. Coleus are not at all fussy about the compost that they require and one that will grow most pot plants successfully is (with certain exceptions) equally suitable for Coleus. To be ideal it should be on the gritty, light side and have a texture which will prevent it from consolidating into a solid lump after a few waterings. It must also have the capacity to retain an adequate reserve of moisture yet at the same time be reasonably well ventilated.

The fertiliser or manure content of the medium should be only moderate. If too much is present the plants will be rank in growth and poor in colour. If the plant food content is too low and the plants do not make a sufficient rate of progress, it is quite easy to add more, but if too much is given in the first place it is quite impossible to take out the excess.

At one time all gardeners mixed their own potting compost, but now it is usual to buy a proprietary ready mixed compost from a merchant or manufacturer.

Amongst the many wholesome and honest mixtures available have always been found those of identical description which, when used, give disappointing results. Composts made from low quality ingredients, especially the loam, produce a final product

E

having a growing power of only a fraction of what it should be. A reliable compost is the first essential for successful growing. John Innes Potting compost, Number 2 or Number 3, obtained from a reputable source, is ideal.

In more recent times plant growing mixtures based on peat have become available. In general, these are satisfactory for many types of plants and give good short term results. Peat, however, possesses neither latent residual fertility nor growing power, and the sustenance available to the plant is added in the form of chemicals. Unfortunately, some of these mixtures contain fertilisers designed to release nitrates continuously. This may be ideal for quick growing green foliage plants, but the continued availability of excess nitrogen is detrimental to the development of good bright colours in Coleus. Peat composts also require to be handled with more intelligence and skill than J.I.P. types. The water absorbing capacity of peat is a valuable quality which can become a serious disadvantage if the peat is over-wetted, particularly when the temperature is low. It is difficult, too, to re-establish a satisfactory moisture quota in such a compost when it has become dry inadvertently.

Preparing one's own potting compost for Coleus is simple and the grower is helped by the fact that, for potting on, unsterilised soil gives results equal to sterilised, the latter consideration depending, of course, upon the soil being wholesome and free from obvious pathogenic organisms and serious weed trouble. The best time to start is in the autumn and early winter. Select a small area of the garden, cover it well with a good dressing of properly made compost or, if you have it, rotted manure. Dig this into the top six inches of soil and leave rough-dug for the frost to work on. Practically any kind of manure will do but if poultry manure is used add 2 ounces of superphosphate of lime per square yard to balance the excess of nitrogen in the manure. The plot will be ready for use as soon as the manure has broken down, decomposing into the structure of the soil. It is not possible to advise precisely how much manure will be needed; this will depend upon the type of soil involved and the state of its fertility. Heavy retentive clay soils require much less than light, open well- ventilated, sandy earths. The latter should be considered as permanently needing additional humus.

Now for the mixing. For a soil or loam-based compost, the three main bulk ingredients are fine granulated horticultural peat, good enriched garden soil and coarse grit. To prepare one bushel (8 gallons) of potting compost, use about two gallons of peat (moistened if necessary), the remaining six being a mixture of the enriched soil and grit. A heavy clay soil may require one part of grit to two of soil, giving a final suitable mix of 2 parts of peat, 2 of coarse grit and 4 of soil. A suitable mixture using sandy soil might be 2 parts of peat and 6 of soil with no grit at all. A handful of a suitable mixture upon being squeezed as hard as possible should be of the texture to just cling together upon releasing the hand. This will hold both water and air, will not pack down too solid nor dry out too quickly. To each bushel of this mixture add 2 ounces of general garden fertiliser in a fine powdered state. Work this into the heap and then add up to 2 ounces of ground limestone per bushel at the grower's discretion if the soil is in need of lime. Turn over the heap several times and pass it through a $\frac{1}{2}$ inch or $\frac{3}{4}$ inch mesh riddle. Before it is used for Coleus it should be brought into the greenhouse to warm up first; Coleus must not be potted into cold compost.

SEED SOWING COMPOST

For sowing Coleus seed an entirely different compost is needed. This should be of a fine texture, with peat to retain moisture and enough grit or coarse sand to create good ventilation. It is important that the soil or loam used should have been correctly sterilised either by steam, electricity or chemicals. A mixture of 2 parts by bulk of fine horticultural peat, 1 part sterilised soil, medium texture and 3 parts of coarse grit is a suitable formula. To each bushel add 1 ounce of general garden fertiliser. If a small quantity only of sowing compost is being prepared, the grower could omit the general fertiliser and use instead a complete liquid fertiliser, watered on at sowing time, according to the manufacturer's instructions. Alternatively, the grower could use one of the proprietary seed sowing composts, using it according to the manufacturer's instruction.

STRIKING COMPOST

For rooting cuttings a successful compost is 2 parts of fine horticultural peat, 1 part of sterilised medium loam or soil and 2 parts of coarse grit. To each bushel add 1½ ounces of general garden fertiliser. Mix the whole thoroughly and put it through a ½ inch mesh riddle. This mixture has an adequate moisture retaining quality for using in the early spring. As the season advances it tends to dry out too quickly. This is corrected by reducing the grit content slightly and substituting with more peat. Rooting cuttings is a growth process and for maximum progress ample oxygen is required which the grower must ensure by allowing as much air to circulate in the compost as possible. A close-textured compact striking compost causes slow rooting.

GROWING FROM SEED

Before the grower sows his seed he must be quite sure that he can maintain the minimum temperature required to ensure easy germination. This is at least 65°F (18°C) but 70°F (21°C) would be much better.

The best time to start is in February or March, making several sowings at intervals of ten to fourteen days or so. If the necessary temperature cannot be provided, sowing should be delayed until the weather becomes warm enough to ensure it. Seed sown after the middle of May will produce plants of small stature only.

Use a clean, preferably new, seed box, place a suitable amount of sterilised seed compost into it, level it off and sow the seed thinly. Cover the seed with a light sprinkling of the same compost, just sufficient to hide it. Water it in carefully, using a fine seed rose on the can. The water must be perfectly clean and hygienic

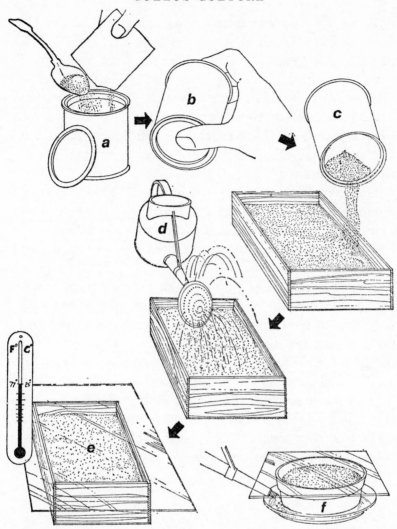

Sowing Coleus seed

In order to ensure even distribution of the seed it is advantageous to mix the Coleus seed together with some fine, dry sand. The sand and seed should be shaken in a tin and then distributed evenly onto the surface of a ready-prepared seed box. Any exposed seed should be covered with a very thin layer of extra sand. The seed box is then watered, covered with a glass sheet, and placed in a minimum temperature of 70°F. A higher temperature is more satisfactory, but the box should be shaded from direct sunlight. Smaller quantities of seed may be sown in a seed pan, which can be placed in a saucer and watered from below.

and at greenhouse temperature. Cheshunt compound or Captan may be used also if desired. If you are using a homemade compost which does not contain an added base fertiliser, use a liquid fertiliser with the initial watering, omitting the Cheshunt compound.

The seed box should be covered with a sheet of glass or a piece of transparent plastic sheeting; place the box on to a reliable hot bed where a suitable temperature can be maintained. Alternatively, a propagating case may be used. A constant moist heat must be maintained during germination. If the temperature fluctuates too often below the minimum, all growth is retarded. The subsequent loss of vigour will permit pre-emergence rotting organisms to become active and cause failure by killing the seeds before they germinate, the grower then wrongly assuming that his seed was poor.

The seedbox should be shaded from the direct sun. If the hot sunshine is caught underneath the glass or plastic covering, the temperature in the confined space will become excessive and this can kill or damage the seeds or damage any emerged radicles or cotyledons. Overheating can be just as dangerous as low temperatures. In ideal conditions and with good seed, the seedlings will appear in six or seven days time. As soon as they are reasonably well germinated they should be uncovered but left in the heat for three or four days longer, still in good light but shaded from any hot sun. After this time they can be moved to a slightly cooler

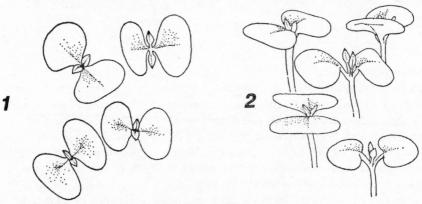

Coleus seedlings shown from above and from the side.

position in the greenhouse, bearing in mind that they are happier above 60°F (16°C) than below it.

Whilst in the seed leaf stage all Coleus look alike and are just plain green except for a few of the very darkest types which may have a little dark brown on their seed leaves. Even some of the black-leaved types start with plain green seed leaves.

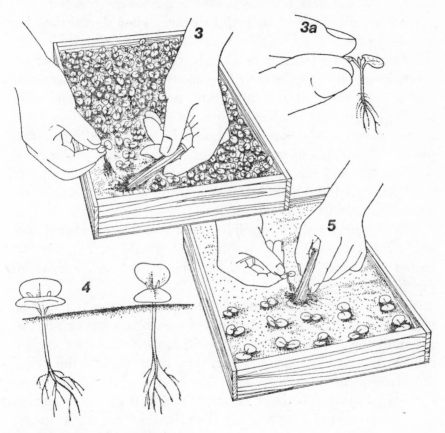

Handling Coleus seedlings

The first illustration (3) shows the thickly-sown box of Coleus seeds. Each seedling should be pricked out using a pointed spatula. The seedlings should be held by the leaf and not by the main stem. The small seedlings should be replanted at a distance of two inches apart each way. Although at first sight this distance between seedlings seems excessive, they very soon grow and require this amount of room.

As soon as the seedlings are large enough to handle safely they should be pricked out to about 2 inches apart each way into J.I.P. No. 2 potting compost. At the time this seems to be rather a wide spacing but the young plants will require it as they are very rapid growers. After pricking out they should be lightly watered-in and the box placed where it can be kept a little warmer for the next few days. This will help the plants to re-cover from the shock of their disturbance. They should then be favoured with a place in the lightest part of the glasshouse but avoiding scorching sunshine. At this stage the only selecting of seedlings which should be done is to discard the obviously weakest and poorest ones, at the same time not confusing them with seedlings which are smaller because they are a day or two later in germinating. The largest, strongest growing seedlings often produce the plants of poorest colours. Usually, the seedlings of medium size and vigour produce the best and brightest plants. Reject any seedlings which have very white stems as these almost always produce feeble plants later.

It is also practically impossible to tell at this stage what shape of foliage the individual seedlings will produce. The narrow croton types and the wavy and frilly kinds all look the same in the tiny leaf stage.

The colours and leaf shapes develop progressively as the little plants put out more and more pairs of true foliage leaves but it is not until the fourth or fifth pairs are formed that their merits can be reasonably assessed. When they have reached this stage of development the grower can then inspect and discard those of unsatisfactory colours or habits. Nothing is gained by being too tender-hearted. Seedlings can be raised quite easily in quantity and the grower should be satisfied only with keeping the best. After the weeding-out has been done the remainder should be potted up.

RAISING PLANTS FROM CUTTINGS

Coleus cuttings may be rooted at any time of the year but the best

Winter Sun. The best golden brown cultivar and an exceptionally good exhibition sort.

Brightness. A very compact cuttings-grown sort which is capable of really living up to its name.

The New Hybrids.
Frilled, deep red

The New Hybrids.
Dark brown specimen

Glory of Luxembourg. Undoubtedly the best cultivar
of its colour. Shy-flowering and good grower, lending
itself well to any training routine.

The New Hybrids.
Uniform warm red-brown

Crimson Ruffles, left, and Glory of Luxembourg, right. Two good subjects in 5″ pots beginning their training for standards.

Cream specimen from The New Hybrids mixed seed strain

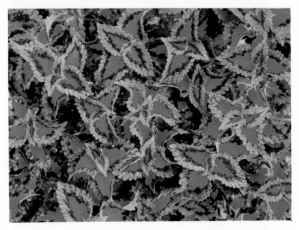

Dunedin. A cultivar with medium-sized leaves. Its semi-trailing habit makes it an excellent subject for a hanging basket. In the late autumn it puts out a mass of beautiful blue flowers, becoming a first-class flowering plant in its own right.

Pastel Rainbow, from the Rainbow Hybrids seed strain.

Beauty. A self-coloured sport from Paisley Shawl. It retains all the good qualities of the parent variety.

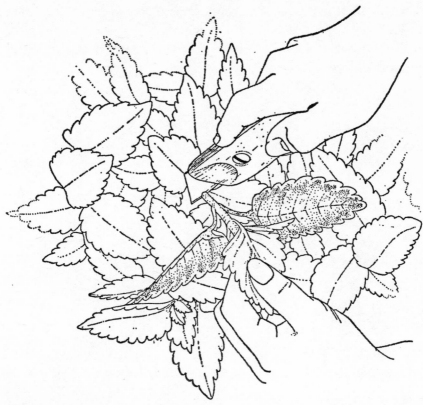

Taking a cutting

Any non-flowering shoot of reasonable vigour may be chosen. The cutting should be from $1\frac{1}{2}''$ to $2''$ in length and may be severed with a sharp knife. The cut need not be made with reference to any joint or node. Coleus cuttings put out roots equally well from any part of the stem.

time to start is from the middle of February in warmer parts to a fortnight or so later in the cooler climates of more northern parts. This will provide enough time to grow good well-furnished plants by mid-summer. The winter is best avoided for rooting the cuttings as the heat required to do so coupled with the short hours of weak daylight tend to produce poor weedy-looking young plants which compare unfavourably with the sturdy vigorous rooted cuttings which can be produced from the month of April onwards. If early plants are particularly required it is best to raise them during the previous autumn, several rooted round the edges of small clay pots, leaving them growing in their inserted state until required. Otherwise it is better to wait until near the vernal equinox before putting in the cuttings.

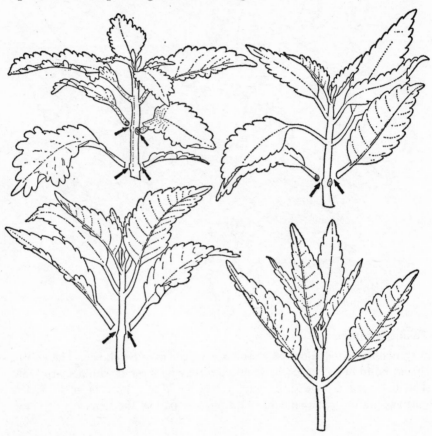

Trimming Coleus cuttings

The first cutting (top left) has had both the bottom pairs of leaves removed as indicated by the arrows. The other two cuttings (top right and bottom left) have had only one pair of leaves removed. The cutting (bottom right) requires no further trimming. It should be noted that it is not essential to trim any of the cuttings to length under a joint or node.

The best type of plant material for cuttings is young, newly-grown, reasonably short-jointed and green in the stem. Old shoots which may have remained on the plant for most of the winter (often white or pale in the stem) take too long to root and produce such feeble plants that they should never be used. Avoid also shoots with highly coloured leaves of mature tint; these, too, are old and slow to root. Reliable cutting material is always green in the stem and leaf. The cuttings need not be more than two inches long from tip to base, preferably with four leaves. It is not necessary to trim them to below or near to a joint; they will root equally well no matter where they are cut. It is only necessary to trim them to a convenient length. Inserted leaves root easily but, as they do not generate growing points, they die after a time.

If the striking conditions are as they should be, the use of synthetic rooting auxins is not usually necessary as they root quite readily without aid. Experience may prove, however, that some cultivars root more slowly than others and these should be treated if they are included in a mixed batch of cuttings all of which are required to be ready for potting together.

Potting up   A seedling being potted into a $3\frac{1}{2}''$ pot –
the minimum practical size for Coleus.

If the grower is unable to prepare a sterile striking compost as described earlier he should buy a reliable proprietary one. The mixture should be placed in the greenhouse to warm up for 24 hours before use and the boxes filled before the cuttings are made. This allows the cuttings to be inserted immediately they are taken and prevents them from wilting before they are planted. They should be inserted about three inches apart each way; that is, about sixteen per square foot. On no account must they be closer than twenty per square foot. If they are, they can so easily be spoiled by becoming drawn when rooted if there is any delay in potting them. Very small quantities of cuttings may be struck around the edges of $3\frac{1}{2}$-inch or 4-inch pots, four or five per pot. When the cuttings have been inserted they should be put in a temperature of about 70°F (21°C) with a bottom heat and watered thoroughly with clean tepid water. A propagating case is ideal but if this is not available, a heated bench is just as effective if the box full of cuttings is simply covered completely over with a clean piece of lightweight plastic sheeting. The cuttings are not in any way hampered by the sheet lying on them. A heavy condensation will appear under the sheeting but this is in no way harmful. The atmosphere and the compost under the cover is maintained in a saturated state and the unrooted cuttings make rapid progress and actually increase in size considerably whilst rooting. Care should be taken to prevent overheating from direct sunshine as described under growing from seeds. A thermometer should be used to check the temperature of the striking medium, enclosing it among the cuttings. If the temperature falls too low, too often, losses will occur from rotting organisms which cause 'staggers' and soft rots of the leaves. The only effective remedy for this condition is to raise the temperature. These temperatures are after all in keeping with the climatology of the plant which has influenced its environmental development.

A first check on the progress of the cuttings may be made about seven days after inserting them. As soon as they begin to grow, the transparent covering over them should be removed promptly. Any delay in doing this will cause the cuttings to become drawn.

A group of cuttings inserted around the edge of a 3½"
pot.
When inserted into a box, the cuttings should be given
more room to grow on.

When the covering is first removed the cuttings will be only
partially rooted and should remain on the heat until they are
rooted fully. With the removal of the covering, the highly saturated atmosphere will become lost and the rooting cuttings may
wilt a little if the weather is bright and warm. At this time they
must be sprinkled or sprayed overhead and covered with shading
for two or three days. Newsprint will serve if nothing more suitable is available.

When they are fully rooted the boxes should be placed on a
bench or shelf at a temperature of about 65°F (18°C). After about
seven days of cooling them down in this way they will be about
ready for potting on. It should also be noted that cuttings inserted
later in the season will reach potting-on stage more quickly than
those inserted earlier.

If the grower has neither the stock nor adequate cutting-
raising facilities, his best course it to buy his cuttings already
rooted in the spring. This is quite the cheapest and easiest way
of meeting the needs of one who wishes to grow a few plants of
named cultivars but who does not wish to have the trouble and

73

expense of maintaining the relatively high minimum winter temperature required to keep the stock plants.

POTTING-UP AND AFTERCARE

For potting-up either seed-raised plants or rooted cuttings a compost should be provided as recommended in the chapter on composts. Ensure that it is at greenhouse temperature before using and that the plants are healthy and sound. The first planting should be into pots of at least $3\frac{1}{2}$ inches (9 cms.) diameter. Put the compost round the roots with moderate firmness. Tight potting will retard the plant's progress whilst a loosely potted plant will dry out too quickly. After potting, the plants should be watered-in and kept at a temperature of about 70°F (21°C) for a few days to help them to overcome the shock of their disturbance.

If the weather is bright and warm at the time, newly potted-up young plants often wilt for several days after their disturbance. Their leaves flag and the soft growing points bend over in an inverted position. As they become established and produce fresh roots they gradually assume normal growth. Beginners sometimes fear that their plants are dying if they do not stand bolt upright at once. The reason for the wilting is that the leaves are transpiring at a rate faster than the disturbed root system can supply moisture. The sap which would normally cause the tissue to remain firm and turgid by internal cell pressure is inadequate, and the soft parts which have no stiff skeleton of hard material (which cells acquire through maturity) wilt and become limp. It is essential to arrest such transpiration by providing temporary shading over the plants. Fine spraying with clean tepid water will also assist during warm bright weather by minimising the loss of moisture from the plants. However, if the weather is dull and cloudy, care must be taken to ensure that the plants do not become too wet or damping-off might easily occur.

The actual progress they will make will be governed by the vigour of the sorts grown, the plant food, the water and the light available to them, and the temperature at which they are grown. Coleus are indeed very rapid growers and quickly make full use of the available plant food. As Shirley Hibberd commented in 1869, 'Plants that grow fast usually require good living'. A March struck cutting of a strong growing sort, could, with suitable treatment become a bush, three feet in diameter and three feet tall by the autumn. A slower growing sort might, under precisely identical conditions, assume only half these proportions. The rate at which they grow should always be borne in mind as they can so easily command all available glasshouse space and still demand more. Because of this, the space between the plants at the initial potting up should not be less than six inches. If the plants are too close for too long, the bottom breaks become smothered and the basal section of the stem becomes drawn, thus frustrating all hopes of developing a short bushy plant.

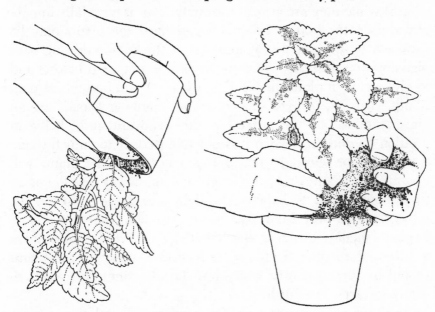

On the left shows the method used to remove the plant from the existing pot.

The right hand illustration shows the plant, together with its root ball being supported in a larger pot while additional soil is firmed in around the roots.

Plants should be re-potted as they require it as the season advances. The need for this is usually indicated by the plant's slowing down in growth and losing its appearance of full well-being. It is better to anticipate this condition and re-pot early rather than allow it to develop fully. The final potting-on of the season usually takes place before late July and the pot size will be determined both by the use which the grower has in mind for the plants and by the individual requirements of particular plants. The usual rule is ' the larger and more vigorous the plant, the larger the pot required'. It will be found that for most general use the 4 inch (10 cms.) size is quite large enough. Pots up to 6 inches (15 cms.) or even larger ones up to 9 inches (22½ cms.) may be used for individual selected plants, such as those intended for Exhibition or Show purposes.

The plants must be kept well-watered during the summer months while they are growing strongly. This is especially important during the hotter, brighter weather or the plants may be damaged by the sun. We mentioned in the section dealing with pigmentation that the grower must also be prepared beforehand to give shade to plants under glass when the sun becomes strong. Blinds, curtains, sprayed or painted on ' Summer Cloud' are all quite suitable but the latter has the disadvantage of being in position on dull days when it is not required. If too much shade is provided or allowed when it is not necessary the plants will become green and drab, the bright colours never developing as they should. How to balance the light and shade is, in the last resort, learned only from experience. The light source available to plants should be such as to enable them to develop uniformly in a balanced manner. If this is not entirely possible, the plants should be turned a little every few days to counteract any tendency towards one-sidedness.

In the earlier stages both the seed-raised and the cutting-raised plants require very similar treatment and as the young potted plants become well-established and are growing away strongly they should be ' stopped' by removing their growing points after about the fifth pair of foliage leaves. With this treat-

Leaf of maroon-red Fantasia type seedling.

Box of Dunedin cuttings, well-rooted and ready for potting on.

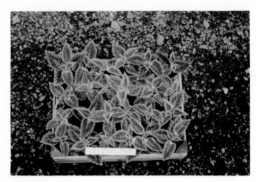

A selection of cuttings, prepared and ready for insertion. It will be noted that the length of stem from the base to the growing point is from about 1½″ to 2″, that the position of the nodes or joints was completely disregarded when trimming them to length and that generally, they have one main pair of leaves with one pair partly grown.

Three well-rooted specimens. They have grown an extra pair of leaves since they were inserted.

Freckles. A most attractive, two-toned cultivar.

Autumn. A compact, sturdy cultivar. Probably the best of its colour.

Autumn Rainbow, from the Rainbow Hybrids seed strain.

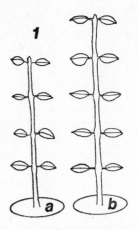

Diagram showing the first step in training a
Coleus into a bush. Remove the tip of the
plant as soon as it can be conveniently done
after either (a) the fourth pair of leaves or (b)
the fifth pair of leaves. (b) is more suitable for
achieving a larger plant.

ment they should branch out freely, producing neat, well-shaped
bushy plants of at least eight side shoots. This single stopping
may suffice for smaller plants in the lesser sized pots, say late in
the season, but for making larger plants in larger pots the side
shoots themselves may be pinched back to two or three pairs
of leaves as they grow long enough. This treatment will produce
plants bearing at least sixteen shoots which may, in their turn,
have their tips removed also. Systematic pinching and trimming
produces plants neat and regular in shape, dense of growth and
of a good size. If particular plants are required for a special
time, say for a show or special occasion, it is best to arrange the
last stopping for about four weeks before the date of the show
to allow time for the pinched off ends of the shoots to become
quite hidden in the mass of new growth.

This systematic stopping, besides producing a shapely plant,
will delay the production of flower spikes for as long as is prac-
ticably possible. Often, seed raised plants are allowed to grow on
until a flower spike develops before any stopping is attempted. By
this time it is nearly always too late to produce the most attractive
type of plant. In general, plants which have been reared from
seed will tend to run into flower although there are exceptions,
notably in 'The New Hybrids' strain which will produce some
plants that are non-flowering during their first year. Plants which
tend to flower readily are best regarded as annuals and should be

discarded in the autumn. Such plants, even when successfully wintered, produce even more flower spikes during their second season.

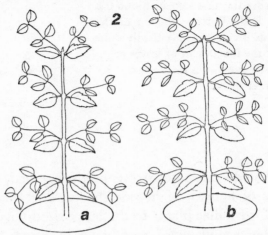

Diagram showing the second step in training a Coleus into a bush. Remove the tips of the side shoots after either (a) their second or (b) their third pair of leaves. (b) is more suitable if a larger plant is intended.

Many of the named cultivars also flower, in varying degrees, but even a single stopping of the plant as described will prevent flower formation for the season in many of them.

In 1968 I was in one of our larger English cities. During my return walk to the car park I saw a coleus plant in the window of a florist's shop. Recognising it as having been reared from seed which we had produced and that it had sported in a most curious fashion, I entered and bought it. 'What do I do with it?' I asked, trying to ease the sales patter. 'Oh,' replied the girl assistant, 'it's a Coleus – all you have to do is just water it.' Nodding, I paid her and left the shop. Continuing on my way I was approached by a group of workmen. One of them, recognising what kind of plant I was carrying, commented to his associates. 'I bet he doesn't know what he's got – ' (pause as we passed each other) '– and I'll tell you something else, he won't keep it. All the leaves will drop off!' Needless to say, they did not, for the plant thrived.

Presumably if our friend and informant had taken home this plant the leaves would, unquestionably, have dropped off! In fact, it is regrettably true that many people who buy a coleus (and other plants, too) find this to be so. But why is this? Why for some people and not for others?

Diagram showing the third step in training a Coleus to produce a bush. Remove the tips of the secondary side shoots after their second pair of leaves. Subsequent training should be aimed at pinching back any wayward shoots and preserving the shape of the plants.

First, we must realise what kind of nature the cultivated coleus has. This beautiful mongreloid creation is really a sub-shrub. With few exceptions it is capable of living for many years. (Rumphius reported that the plant which he described as Majana Aurea lived for at least fifteen years in Ceram.) The stems of the ordinary coleus plant will become woody and hard as it matures,

79

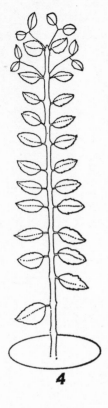

Diagram showing the first step in training a Coleus to produce a standard. The plant is encouraged to grow tall and straight. Remove all side shoots but retain the leaves. The plant is shown with the tip removed at the required height and the top four shoots retained to produce the head. Note that they have been stopped after only the first pair of leaves.

In this diagram the plant has had the leaves of the main stems removed and the secondary side shoots have been stopped after their second pair of leaves. Subsequent stoppings are made at the discretion of the grower.

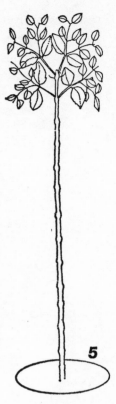

4

5

similar to a fuchsia or lantana. The leaves are soft and deciduous and therefore detach themselves and drop off after full maturity. During the growing season the shedding of old leaves from a vigorous healthy plant should not cause disfigurement as the plant will be in such a state of development that the loss will be insignificant. The plant is never perpetually denuded of most of its leaves unless it is either unhealthy or is in a suffering condition. Let us consider the process of normal leaf shedding as this will assist us in mastering our problem.

In deciduous plants there forms during development and growth, near to the point of union of the leaf petiole and the shoot that bears it, a layer of specialised cells. This is called the abscission layer; it consists of cells arranged in a very narrow band only a few cells thick and stretches completely across the

80

whole width of the petiole, involving all the cells except the vascular bundles, and its purpose is to cause the leaf to drop off when it becomes old and unproductive. This layer begins to form before leaf maturity. Shortly before the leaf falls, changes take place in the cell walls. The middle lamella between adjacent cells breaks up and dissolves; cells become isolated and therefore perish. The vascular bundles still remain operative and it is by the mechanical strength of these alone that the leaf remains attached. Ultimately, however, they snap and the leaf drops off.

In very young coleus leaves there is no abscission layer. According to Sampson who studied this problem as long ago as 1918,[1] the abscission layer in coleus is usually initiated in the third pair of leaves below the terminal bud. When these become the fourth pair, the leaf is usually fully grown in size and growth ceases. Development of the abscission layer continues however, and as the pair of leaves in question forms the sixth pair down, the layer is usually complete. Note that the layer is initiated before leaf maturity and still continues to develop for quite some time afterwards. Sampson reported that all the leaves from the third pair downwards could be made to fall prematurely by subjecting the plant to a shock such as exposure to ethylene gas, or by allowing the soil to become parched, followed by excess of water. The experimental plants were given glasshouse conditions, grown in 4" pots and just commencing abscission of their eighth pair of leaves.

Sampson's study was made of the chemical aspects of coleus leaf abscission. In his conclusions he pointed out that unknown factors were involved which posed problems then unresolved. In the half century which has elapsed since, new knowledge has shown that one major factor is the role that plant auxins play in the process. We now know that the balance between auxin levels in both leaf and shoot is decisively critical. Speaking in a very general way for reasons of simplicity, we may say that plants produce chemical auxins which regulate various functions of growth and development. Relatively larger quantities are produced in the active growing point and are passed back down

81

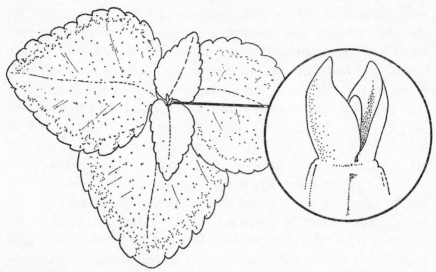

Apical bud
The shoot growing point (Apical bud) is an important centre where growth regulators (auxins) are produced. These are passed down the shoot and check the development of side shoots for some distance below. 'Stopping' removes the Apical bud. The side shoots then develop. These side shoots in turn carry their own Apical buds, and these in their turn must be removed if the plants are to be persuaded to become neat and bushy.

the growing plant dispersing into tissues en route. Sunlight, also, causes a dispersal of some auxins. Different concentrations of auxins will either stimulate or depress various functions of plant development and growth, i.e. strong concentrations found near growing tips depress bud development (except apical) but stimulate cell elongation. A concentration which will stimulate root development is not sufficient to stimulate stem cell elongation.

If the concentration of auxin is higher in the leaf than in the shoot bearing it, abscission will not usually take place, but as soon as the balance is reversed the leaf will detach if an abscission layer has already formed. The reversal of auxin balance between leaf and stem is hastened if the plant is subjected to a shock causing the vigour of the plant to decline. The leaves will then produce less auxin themselves, particularly the older ones, and abscission can then be almost immediate, especially with these older ones which have fully developed abscission tissue. Younger leaves, producing more auxin than older ones contribute towards the abscission of the older ones.[2,3,4]

The plant may be subjected to many conditions which could cause a shock. Draughts, whether hot or cold, can cause abscission very quickly. The drying out of the soil can also bring about shock by causing the minute feeding roots to wither. The moisture intake is thus impaired and the plant wilts and suffers. This condition is often followed by a period of over-watering (stimulated by the owner's anxious concern). The root ball will then become soggy in consequence of air being driven out by excess of water retained in the interstices between soil particles. A sick plant, already damaged in its root system, cannot dry up the excess moisture by evaporating it through the process of growing and the plant collapses. A constant level of just sufficient moisture is essential for steady growth. In maintaining this, appreciation will have to be made of all the factors governing the plant's requirements in relation to the prevailing conditions as each day demands.

One of the main reasons for persistent leaf dropping in town and city areas is the presence of coal gas. Either the leakage of gas or the presence of combustion fumes can be very harmful. Many other kinds of plants, too, are susceptible to this. It will be remembered that Sampson used ethylene gas to cause leaf dropping in his abscission experiments. Ethylene is present in coal gas and is not destroyed during combustion but remains present in the fumes. Coal gas has also been used for its ethylene content for the ripening of green tomato fruit. The gas stimulates the ripening of tissue. The ethylene content of natural gas as compared with coal gas is only about 1/50th and presumably this will not be as damaging as coal gas, the ethylene content of which could be as high as 5%. At the time of writing the results of further studies dealing with the effects of ethylene is being published. One report indicates that the levels of auxin in leaf and apical bud tissues of coleus is altered by the presence of ethylene.[5]

83

It will be noted that upon coleus that shed their leaves prematurely the top two or three pairs still remain attached. This is because at this stage of growth no abscission layer has formed and therefore separation cannot take place. This last comment also links up with the practice of pruning and frequently stopping coleus during their growing season. Single-stemmed plants can all too easily assume the shape of a miniature palm tree with a tuft of foliage at the top. By stopping the main stem and pinching out the growing points of the side shoots as they appear, the apical buds are removed, thus assisting towards a more favourable auxin balance between leaf and shoot. A greater number of leaves borne by a frequently stopped plant will therefore not have initiated abscission layers at any particular time as compared with a plant less frequently stopped. One other feature about plant management in general which should be more widely understood is that the main reason for many kinds of plants not growing bushy quickly is that the auxin produced by the apical bud in the main growing point is depressing the development of the axillary buds. After the growing tip has been removed, side shoots will then sprout.

1 *Botanical Gazette* 66. p. 32-53, 1918. Sampson. *Chemical changes accompanying abscission in C. blumei*

2 *Proceedings of National Academy of Science, Washington,* vol. 22 p. 254-259. D. La Rue. *The effect of Auxin on the abscission of petioles*

3 *American Journal of Botany.* vol. 42. p. 594-603. Jacobs. *The physiological basis of the abscission-speeding effect of intact leaves*

4 *American Journal of Botany.* vol. 40, p. 273-276. 1953. Whitmore and Jacobs. *Studies on Abscission*; also p. 276-280. Rossetter and Jacobs, *Studies on Abscission*

5 *Plant Physiology* 46. Supplement 20. 1970. Valdovinos and Ernest. *Effects of Ethylene on Auxin Metabolism in Coleus Blumei*

5

Towards Perfection

Training plants into different shapes:
  (a) *pyramid*
  (b) *standard*
  (c) *fan*

Uses of Coleus:
  (a) *in the home*
  (b) *conservatory*
  (c) *hanging baskets*

List of named cultivars
Growing for competition
Summer bedding-out

TOWARDS PERFECTION

Although the bush is the usual Coleus plant shape generally seen, other shapes can also be grown. The simplest is the pyramid. Use a variety which is vigorous in growth, naturally bushy and slow to flower. Paisley Shawl, Royal Scot, Walter Turner and Carnival are suitable. The plant should be potted up as early in the season as practicable, if possible using an unstopped autumn-struck young plant. Give it good treatment and let it grow unstopped, being careful not to shade the base of the plant or it will not develop properly. Tie up the plant to a cane, taking care to ensure that the swelling stem does not become 'strangled' by the ties; re-tie as it becomes necessary. As the basal breaks appear, tie them to small canes placed as near to horizontal as is possible. Keep stopping back the side shoots, so that the plant bushes out into a dense and solid form broad at the base and pointed at the top. The growth should be stopped at a suitable height. Cut off any protruding ends of canes. The canes themselves will become lost amongst the leaves. A successful first year plant might attain a height of two and a half feet and two feet through at the base. Second and third year plants easily make specimens four feet high and three feet through.

Two other shapes which look very attractive are the Half-Standard and the Full-Standard. They are always admired whenever they are seen and are quite easy to produce. The Half-Standard can be produced in one season and improves during the second season. The Full-Standard will necessarily require two seasons for developing into a good specimen. Named cultivars are necessary as it is not possible to develop a standard head on a short stem which terminates in a flower spike.

To grow a Half-Standard, an early struck cutting of a suitable strong growing sort should be potted on and kept growing strongly and unstopped until it is about two feet tall. Extra fertiliser should be used as a top dressing and while the stem is being grown it is not necessary to be concerned about the colour of the leaves, only that the plant makes maximum growing progress. Keep it secured to a cane and ensure that it develops perfectly straight.

As it grows, the side shoots should be removed and when it has attained the required height, which will probably be during June, the plant should be stopped and the head built up from the top four joints on the main stem, allowing the eight axial shoots from these four joints to develop and removing any still remaining ones below. These top eight shoots should have their tips removed after two pairs of leaves and following shoots likewise, with discretion, to build up a dense, solid 'head'. If the stopping-back

86

of the shoots is delayed, a solid head will not be forthcoming as new growth will be produced on the extremities, leaving an open lattice of shoots in the centre.

As the head is developing towards its full state, withhold the application of any more fertiliser or the foliage will not produce good strong colours.

To grow a Full-Standard the chosen sort must be allowed to grow upwards, making one stem only for the whole of the first season. An excellent cultivar for this purpose is Glory of Luxembourg. It can reach a height of four feet by October or November having passed through the production of thirty pairs of leaves.

Treat the plant exactly as described for the Half-Standard but keep it growing by liberal treatment. If a flower spike appears, this will limit the height to which the particular stem can be grown and the gardener will have to be content. If a flower shows itself, it should be removed as soon as conveniently possible, together with the top two pairs of leaves. The building up of the head should then begin in exactly the same manner as with the Half-Standard. If the stem is tall enough without having shown signs of flowering, the top should be removed as the required height is reached and the head built up from the top four joints as described earlier. The grower must anticipate this particular phase of growth and not remove any of the shoots which should be left to develop. Quickly growing stems of standards usually appear ridiculously thin, weak and weedy, even when quite tall. The stems will, however, develop astonishingly in girth as the season passes, becoming stiff and stout. The ties must be watched most carefully or the stems might be ruined by becoming constricted. The owner of a small greenhouse should remember that the plant he is planning to produce could become too big for his greenhouse by the autumn! As the autumn closes, the heads should already be starting to form. During the over-wintering stage, stopping-back and shaping can continue as growth will permit. The head will continue to grow and it is very important that the branches composing it should be securely tied up to an internal cross lattice and to one another, to avoid breakages.

Re-pot the standard in January or February. This is important. Unless good growing conditions are provided, the breaks will not appear. Flushes of new growth can be induced through the application of successive doses of fertiliser but such treatment ultimately produces an inferior plant established in impoverished compost with the poor condition of the plant becoming increasingly evident in the middle of the growing season. This poor condition also predisposes plants towards flowering.

It is usual to produce a Full-Standard with a good head of eighteen inches in diameter by about early July in the second season, that is, after about sixteen months of growing time.

Another simple and attractive shape is the Fan. This is essentially a bush in which the shoots on two opposite sides have been pinched completely back, thereby producing two flat sides. Large plants of this shape require a number of canes arranged in a fan shape for support.

THE USES OF COLEUS IN THE HOME

Coleus make excellent decorative plants for the home and will thrive in most dwelling houses where the temperature range is adequate.

Under average conditions, the earliest time to start bringing Coleus into a house which is not centrally heated is generally during the month of May. From this time onwards they should grow freely until the autumn when, after a period in which they make less progress, the English winter causes the plants to succumb about late November.

With central heating Coleus can be grown at any time of the year and although they are less attractive during the darker period of the winter, they provide bright colour for seven or eight months out of the twelve. One of the most favoured situations is the window ledge. This, with certain reservations, can be ideal. A westerly, northerly or easterly aspect is quite suitable during the summer because it will avoid exposing the plant to the fading effects of bright sunlight. For the winter, a southerly aspect is to be preferred because the plant would be more successful with the extra light and warmth which the sun would provide. If a southerly window is the only one available, the plants must be positioned away from the window at times when damage might occur through sunlight fading the colours. When the temperature outside is lower than that inside the room, the inside air in contact with the glass loses heat rapidly and causes a down draught. The concentration of cold air which collects on a window-ledge as the descending cold air drains downwards will cause shock to many plants, and Coleus certainly cannot thrive under these conditions. At no time should the plants be in a draught nor should they be left inadvertently on the outside of curtains when drawn, especially in cold weather. Double-glazed windows minimise this problem.

During the summer, Coleus will succeed in porches, halls, glassed-in house extensions or sun lounges and many other situations where sufficient light can be given. If the light is inadequate the plants will become weedy and the colours insipid and a fresh situation must be provided quickly. The plants are better not to be placed close to a wall or large object permanently or the growth will develop one-sided. Also, these plants are seen to better effect when they are below the eye level and in good light. The plants are not seen to full effect if they are placed where they offer only a silhouette, even though the leaves may be bright and attractive. If such a situation is the only one available, the lighter coloured sorts are the best.

Coleus are also extremely effective for providing colour to mixed groups of house plants in troughs and mixed plantings but the gardener must always be watchful that the plants have sufficient room in which to grow or they will quickly become drawn and smaller plants will be smothered.

Coleus in the home look particularly well when displayed individually. This is the only way to do justice to a well-grown specimen. The pot should be clean and placed in a plant pot container or on a saucer. This should be large enough to allow the pot to sit firmly upon the bottom and not to be held up with a space underneath. When water is given to the plant it should be poured into the top of the pot, any small quantity that runs through being retained in the saucer and absorbed by the plant later. This must not be interpreted, however, as permitting the pot to stand with its lower portion permanently submerged or the roots will quickly go rotten and the plant will die.

THE USES OF COLEUS IN CONSERVATORY AND GLASSHOUSE

The best place of all in which to grow Coleus is the glasshouse. If sufficient heat is provided by maintaining a minimum temperature of 60°F (16°C), they are capable of being grown quite easily for the whole of the year. A greenhouse of almost any shape will suffice but a vital factor in greenhouses fitted only with benches is the distance from the surface of the bench to the glass above, as this limits the maximum height to which the plants may be grown. Where space and height is not a problem, Coleus can be grown several feet high and as much through. *The Gardeners' Chronicle* of October 24th 1868, mentioned a plant growing at Broomfield Lodge, Chelmsford as being ' . . . a perfect pyramid, about nine feet high, and nearly as much through at the bottom.' Initially, the plants will require spacing out at four per square foot, and will quickly require re-spacing to about two per square foot. Trying to grow too many plants in too little space will ultimately spoil all of them.

If the gardener wishes to enjoy and appreciate his plants where he grows them – in the greenhouse – a low staging or bench is best, about two feet high with a low tiering at the back if the bench is situated along the side of the greenhouse but down the centre of the bench if it has a path on all its sides. Standards may be grown standing on the floor during the summer months but not during the winter time as this is likely to be the coldest place and fatal root-rots would ensue. Standards can be positioned interspaced, with other plants underneath, provided that they do not cause too much shade.

The procumbent forms such as Picturatum and Lord Falmouth can be given semi-permanent positions at the front of
groups and along the front of benches, being allowed to creep
along and to trail over the edge and downwards.

Coleus will add colour and arrange very well with almost any
other type or kind of foliage or flowering plant provided that
their climatic requirements are compatible at the time. The light-
coloured varieties such as Buttermilk, White Gem, Sunset and
Lemondrop are especially valuable and give to mixed groups and
arrangements an essential contrast in colour, design and form.
In recent years Coleus have been used increasingly in floral art.
For this purpose the self-colours are considered the most useful –
whites, yellows, browns and blacks. A supply of Coleus material
for this purpose is best provided by growing plants specially for
the purpose as the continual removal of shoots from plants grown
for decoration spoils their appearance.

HANGING BASKETS

One way of achieving a very striking decorative effect with
Coleus is to use them in indoor hanging baskets. The best kinds
for this purpose are those of slender growth and branching habit.
The narrow leaved 'croton' types make excellent subjects and
provide the gardener with a most distinctive quick-growing
spectacle. The procumbent types like Lord Falmouth, Picturatum
and Dunedin are also very good for this purpose. Different sorts
may be planted in one basket but generally one variety per basket
gives a better effect and for a larger display, a number of baskets
can be combined. Other plants may be planted with Coleus in
the basket if desired, but these would have to be chosen with care
as they will have to be capable of growing in competition with
the Coleus.

The type of basket which has a permanent drip tray is specially
suitable for use in the home as one of the disadvantages of the
moss-lined wire baskets is that before they can be thoroughly
watered they must be taken down and removed to a position

where they can drain off before being returned to their places. Any size of basket may be used; as a guide, twelve rooted cuttings would be suitable for a ten inch basket. Four would be planted through the sides of the basket, spaced out about two inches below the edge of the rim; four more alternated, planted inside the rim and the remainder planted in the centre of the basket.

The compost for filling is exactly the same as that used for potting. The plants will require stopping after about six pairs of leaves have formed and later pinching or trimming to create a balanced uniform shape. While the basket is developing, see that it is not over-shadowed by other plants or by walls or it will become unbalanced in shape. Turn it round periodically to help it to grow uniformly.

If the soil shows signs of exhaustion, a little general garden fertiliser may be given. The basket should, if made up in the spring, last until the late autumn, but it is best to discard it when its condition declines. In suitably warm quarters, however, the period of usefulness can be extended until well into the winter. As it is normally quite impractical to rejuvenate a hanging basket, the best thing to do is to empty it out and start again, preferably with new young plants. Any plants which may be retained and used again must be cut back severely to make them bush out from the base. Baskets of Coleus are very attractive but they must be used with intelligence and care, remembering that they are not able to stand the rigours of wind blasting and inclement weather.

Some of the pendulous varieties have flowers of a bright gentian blue, Rob Roy and Dunedin especially so. Baskets planted with these kinds produce very attractive and distinctive displays in the late autumn and early winter.

NAMED CULTIVARS OF MERIT

The following list of named cultivars contains the best and most reliable kinds in British horticulture at the present time. Some of these have been known as universal popular favourites for many years and their naming can be regarded as authentic. Other

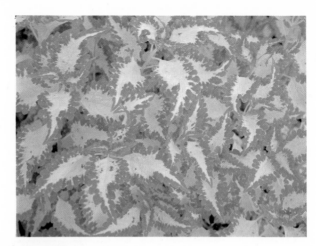

Buttermilk. Probably the best cultivar of its colour.

Salmon Croton. The best narrow-leaved cultivar of its colour and especially useful as a hanging basket subject.

Vulcan. A selection of E. W. King & Co.

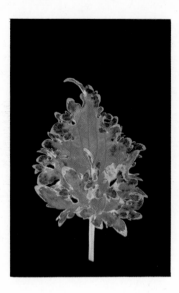

Leaf of Fantasia type seedling notable for its fringed development at the base of the leaf blade.

An arrangement of leaves showing how some Coleus cultivars can produce a range of new sorts, some useful, others useless.

The primary parent is Paisley Shawl, second from the right on the top row, having a green centre speckled with brown and a cream band around the edge speckled with red.

To the right of Paisley Shawl is a form in which the green and cream have changed places. A plant of this kind is less striking than the original. To the left of Paisley Shawl is the all-red sport, Beauty; the red speckles of the parent have expanded into a skin which covers both sides of the leaf.

To the left of Beauty is a form in which the dark brown and red have changed places. Again, less striking as a plant than the original.

To the left again, a form of Beauty which has lost all capacity to display any red.

On the bottom row at the extreme left is a leaf which is half Paisley Shawl and half Beauty.

Next to it is a form which has lost all its green pigment and is incapable of a separate existence if taken from the parent plant.

On the extreme right, bottom row, is a form which is uniform green with brown speckles.

To its left, a form which is uniform green down one half and Paisley Shawl down the other.

There are still other variations but these were not available when this picture was taken.

Leaf of Redfern, one of the new Fantasia type cuttings-grown varieties.

kinds, however, are known under different names in different parts of the country. Unfortunately there is not, as yet, a register of cultivars as is the case with some other plants such as dahlias, roses or chrysanthemums, nor a Coleus Society to keep an eye on the situation. A number of popular sorts have been raised and named by ourselves so we can vouch for the authenticity of their names.

Autumn, reddish brown, maturing to a bright uniform chestnut colour. Short-jointed and compact in habit.

Beauty, dark purplish brown leaf centre, the edge turning bright red. A dark sport of Paisley Shawl.

Brightness, a vivid bronze-chestnut, edged with pale yellow-green. The most striking example of its colour so far. It has medium vigour and a very bushy, sturdy habit.

Buttermilk, a creamy white centre with a mid-green serrated edge, a popular variety which makes a large bushy plant very easily.

Carnival, medium sized leaves of medium green splashed with red, white and brown. A vigorous variety with a neat, spreading habit.

Crimson Ruffles, beetroot red, veined with bright red. Frilled edges, tipped with bright green. A strong growing reliable sort, suitable for exhibition.

Firebrand, leaf centre bright crimson shading out to a red-brown border. The leaf edges are scalloped yellow-green. The habit is vigorous, bushy and sturdy.

Freckles, a light yellow-green, splashed all over with several shades of a light golden and a bright medium brown. A very unusually coloured plant of medium vigour.

Glory of Luxembourg, chocolate brown with a yellow-green edge. A very reliable and popular kind. Excellent for standards and for exhibition use.

Kentish Fire, orange-bronze medium-sized narrow leaves with anastomose veination. The crenations are pale green, the habit is bushy and of medium vigour.

G

Klondike, a uniform red-gold, makes an exceptionally brilliant and striking plant when well-grown. It needs to be well stopped to promote the best bushy habit.

Lemondrop, a clear attractive pale yellow. Makes an upright plant, vigorous and branching.

Paisley Shawl, the leaf centre is dark green speckled with dark brown, the edge turning cream speckled with red. Makes a good, bushy plant.

Pineapple Beauty, yellow with a red-brown blotch on the base of the leaf by the stalk. An excellent bushy and branching habit and makes a large, dense plant, flowering only rarely.

Royal Scot, one of the most brilliantly coloured varieties. The centre of the leaf is dark brown edged with bright red. The edge of the leaf is a bright golden yellow. Its habit is extremely sturdy, bushy and branching.

Scarlet Ribbons, long pointed leaves with red centres surrounded with brown, edged dark green. A strong, vigorous sort.

Sunbeam, a light yellow with a cream centre to the leaf. One of the easier varieties to grow.

Treales, ovate leaves, crimson centres bordered chocolate, edged and veined with light green. Makes an excellent specimen for the show bench.

Walter Turner, leaf centre crimson-maroon, edged with yellow. A vigorous fine sort. Good for the show bench.

Winter Sun, a handsome light golden brown of medium vigour and a bushy habit.

GROWING FOR COMPETITION

Growing plants to perfection for the competitive classes at Horticultural Shows is a special challenge to the grower and makes great demands upon his skill. For this purpose, only the best and most perfect specimens are worth entering. To achieve this class of perfection the grower must have a feeling for the plants and the insight to select and rear only those which are capable of producing the fine specimens required. Possibly, the grower has been attracted towards showing by having earlier seen exhibition plants and has understood the techniques involved, but he must also be quite conversant with the meaning and interpretation of the requirements for the particular class as specified in the Show Schedule. It may sound fatuous and unnecessary advice to say that the plants must always be staged to comply with the rules laid down in the Show Schedule, but some exhibitors are passed by at judging time or even objected to by other exhibitors simply because they have failed to study the Show Authority's printed rules. All kinds of misunderstandings arise as a result of ambiguity. For instance, some Shows specify the maximum size of pot permitted, others simply state 'pot'. Some authorities interpret the term 'pot' as meaning any kind of container for a growing plant whilst others mean a 'plant pot'. The practice in some parts of planting several plants together in one pot to ensure a bushy potful in less time than if a single specimen were used, might pass if entered as a 'pot of Coleus' but not where a schedule stated 'Coleus plant in a pot' or 'one Coleus'. The exhibitor should also study the awards in relation to the judges, and if possible seek advice and reasons as to why his entries were not as successful as he had hoped.

Plants raised from seed are often seen entered in Coleus classes and this type of plant constitutes the majority of entries at smaller shows. Although fair-sized specimens can be produced from suitable seed sown very early in the season, seed-grown plants are limited in stature and need smaller pots to compensate for this; the end product is at a disadvantage when shown against select named types. It is important that suitable varieties be chosen, for some are very much better for the purpose than others. Some kinds grow larger and bushier and are much less likely to develop flower spikes than the seed-grown sorts. Earlier in this book is a list of named cultivars with descriptions and comments on their suitability for exhibition purposes.

An excellent foundation for an exhibition plant would be an autumn-struck cutting rooted in September. Plants of this description are practically never offered in commerce and the grower must rely on producing them himself. Good-sized bushy specimens in six- to ten-inch pots can be obtained in ten months time with this class of young rooted plants. An even better foundation for a first-class exhibition plant would be a plant in good condition in its second year. Such a plant could quite easily become a compact plant three feet through and four feet high when sixteen months or so old. Plants grown for exhibition must have priority in the growing routine and must have all the space they need. The sort chosen should be one which will provide ample colours and should be eye-catching and striking. The habit of the plant should be dense and compact, produced by frequent systematic stopping and pinching. Whatever the shape, it should be as uniform and symmetrical as possible with a minimum of leafless parts of branches showing. The most favoured shape is the bush, grown as circular as possible. With some sorts the diameter will be greater than the height while in others the opposite is the case. The writer has observed that no matter how large a space a plant fills, sheer size is usually a lesser consideration when judged. This does not mean that size is not important. It is. One of the most firmly established rules applied to horticulture where size is not specified is that 'A good big 'un always beats a good little 'un'. Therefore the exhibitor must aim at producing the largest possible plants, but not at the expense of well-shaped habit and good striking colour.

Stake all large plants to prevent damage occurring, by inserting a strong cane up the middle of the plant, as Coleus are often very brittle and snap easily. When the plant becomes larger it will be necessary to put thin canes to each of the principal branches, tying them securely and individually. A strong, effective lattice can be involved which is obscured by the plant as it develops. Subsequent tying should be neatly and carefully done without marring the plant's appearance. Never loop a string full circle round a branch. The constriction will cause a weak part which will later snap, causing the loss of the branch and spoiling the appearance of the plant.

Details about the stopping of Coleus in general is given in the section under 'Culture'. An early struck cutting will allow for a greater number of pinchings than a later struck one during training and shaping, thus producing a better shape. The grower should bear in mind that the last pinching should be not later than four weeks before the plant will be required, thereby allowing new growth to hide the severed ends of the branches. This last pinching is a good time to remove any shoot ends which are obviously producing flower spikes and also to make any final corrections to the shape of the plant.

The compost used throughout is exactly the same as that required by other coleus but because of the extra growth and size of exhibition plants, a little extra fertiliser will be needed. In the early stages, exhibition plants can be given fertiliser without the grower being concerned about their final colours. At this stage it is of first importance to produce the best possible foundation for a large bushy plant. Later on, fertiliser should be given in small amounts at frequent intervals but should be discontinued at about four weeks before the plants are due for exhibiting or the colours may not be fully developed.

Getting the plants ready for a show is best done in good time, at least several days beforehand, so that last minute alterations are minimised. Make sure that all the plants are securely tied; the branches are brittle and will crack easily if they are not adequately supported. Next, wash all the pots thoroughly, including the undersides. Dirty pots lose marks. Stained or discoloured pots can be improved in appearance by rubbing with red ochre or concrete colorant, using a moist cloth. If show authorities require the pots to be covered in some way when staged, moss or other material should be obtained and sorted, ready for use.

Before the actual journey is made the plants must be wrapped to prevent chafing and rubbing. The best material for this purpose is polythene; it is much kinder to the plants than most papers. The wrapping also reduces the diameter of the plants and releases tension on the branches. It also facilitates their manipulation into and out of cars or vans and through small doorways.

97

Standard plants are best tethered inside the vehicle with strings fore, aft and to each side, thus preventing the head from whipping when the vehicle jolts. The carrying of plants about to and from shows tends to spoil their appearance. Leaves become broken and marked, and colours fade. Sometimes they become badly drawn or lean towards one side. Obviously, such plants will need time to recuperate before they can be used again for show purposes. This necessitates growing sufficient plants to enable some to rest while others are being used. Badly drawn plants are best cut well back to create fresh growth.

When the plants reach the show, make sure that they are staged in the correct place as allocated and in the right classes. They should be adequately watered. If the cultivar's name or seed strain is known, display it on a small white card at the base of the pot.

Most plants look best when viewed from a particular position depending upon which side is facing the viewer. Make sure, by turning the plants round a little at a time, that the best sides show to the front. This may help, but not so much with the judge who lifts the plants on to the ground and walks round them to reach his verdict.

COLEUS FOR SUMMER BEDDING-OUT

Coleus are used for bedding-out in Britain in localities and situations which have more favoured climates. Even so, they cannot be relied upon as a source of colour for every summer, as in poor seasons they become drab and spoiled. Britain's climate is far removed from that of the South-West Pacific and gardeners should remember this as they plan their displays.

The best situations are those with an aspect which is sheltered from strong winds and exposure. The soil should be light, in good heart and well-drained; what is often called 'early earth'.

The best displays are those in which the plants are first reared in clay pots, incorporating second and third year specimens trained into special shapes as centre-pieces, with smaller ones in support, forming a 'foil'. The plants should be well-hardened in a frame and given plenty of air as occasion allows, in readiness for planting out, complete in their pots, as the weather permits, choosing a spell of settled warm weather, preferably after mid June. Clay pots are more suitable than plastic ones for this purpose as the latter, if used, insulate the pot-ball from the surrounding soil thereby preventing the plant from drawing upon it for sustenance.

The compost used for growing the plants for this purpose should be only moderately rich. Aim at keeping the growth hard, as this will help the plants to survive inclement conditions with less damage.

Unless it is known that a particular locality is suitable for these plants outside, it would be best to be cautious. Most low altitude areas of the southern counties of England are accepted as being generally suitable but our experience is that the English summer northwards of the southern Midlands is liable to be too cold. *The Gardeners' Chronicle*, September 23rd 1865, p. 891, commented, 'On cold soils the Coleus remains in sickly green and yellow and starved condition throughout the season . . . at Chatsworth . . . (the) Coleus is useless.'

If the plants will be required again for stock making or for use in the following season, care must be taken not to let them become damaged in the early autumn by becoming rotten through cold and wet or, worst still, frosted. Lift the plants into heat in good time for over-wintering.

6

Diseases of Coleus

Aphis
Caterpillar
Mealy bug
Scale insect
White fly
Root knot eelworm
Chrysanthemum eelworm
Spider mite
Botrytis and soft rots

DISEASES OF COLEUS

One of the good points of Coleus is that although they are capable of suffering from a number of pests and diseases, they are not particularly prone to any of them. Insect pests are not normally drawn to them and if the temperature is maintained within the acceptable range they are very resistant to fungal and bacterial rots.

The most common insect affecting Coleus is the aphis. Several types appear on occasions at different times of the season, but they never build up into masses such as are seen on roses or carnations. The infestation is generally slight, usually in the growing

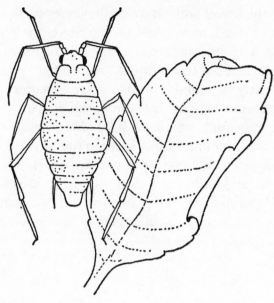

Aphides

These are probably the best known of all plant pests. The commonest are the Greenfly and Blackfly. They are sucking insects and their feeding action distorts leaves and shoots and produces a mottled effect. Control of the pests can be effected by fumigating or spraying with nicotine.

points of shoots. The first indication is that the young unfolding leaves are developing in a distorted fashion, spoiling the appearance of the plant. Flower spikes are sometimes infected, especially in the winter on the flowering species. The cure is simple. Spray the plants with nicotine, pyrethrum or any other aphicide.

Several types of caterpillars can be a source of trouble to Coleus. First, there is the large solitary cutworm type which hides during the day and feeds by night. One individual can spoil several plants in a few nights by eating large holes in the leaves. Another form appears in small colonies of upwards of a dozen or so, progressing from plant to plant. The damage is similar to that caused by the cutworm type but the holes are smaller in size. Sometimes small colonies of very minute caterpillars work

underneath the leaves and eat away the under surface only, causing patches of dead, brown leaf to appear on the upper surface.
This damaged tissue can become the seat of rotting if the humidity is high and the temperature low. Damage usually appears
first during early June and it is best to give a routine spray as soon
as June arrives, with any safe preparation which will control
caterpillars, repeating at intervals of three weeks or so. Small
slugs and snails sometimes cause holes in the leaves. The creatures
are not easily seen and often are not suspected. They generally
feed by night and will crawl to the topmost leaves and shoots.
Slime trails upon the affected plants will indicate that the trouble
is due to these creatures. Sprinkle slug pellets amongst the plants
to eradicate them.

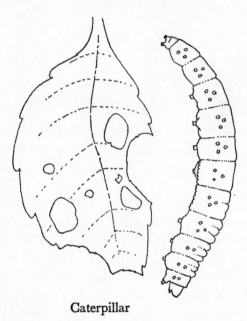

Caterpillar

A more serious pest is Mealy Bug. This trouble is often passed
round on infected plants and when once established in a greenhouse it can be very difficult to eradicate. Adult specimens are
about one-fifth of an inch long, oval in shape and light grey in
appearance. At this stage they are very lethargic and generally

remain in one place on the plants for hours at a time. Younger specimens are very tiny indeed, often being invisible to the naked eye. What they lack in size is more than compensated for by their increased agility and mobility and they move readily from one part of the plant to another. The pest usually gets very close into the angles of stems and leaves; sometimes small ones will shelter in the angles formed by veins, lying close and unobtrusive. Ovisacs of stringy, airborne, downy material cause this pest to spread quickly and it will hide in any small crevice, such as cracks in dead bark, staging boards and boxes, and will even

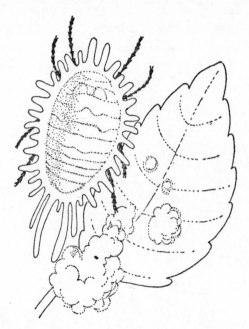

Mealy Bug

This small sap-sucking insect is covered with a white waxy covering. It is a common pest in some old greenhouses. It can hide in the soil and feed upon the roots of potted plants, where it can remain undetected until the plants turn yellow, wilt and often die. The pest can be eradicated by spraying them and watering the soil with either a Malathion or Diazinon insecticide mixed to the maker's instructions.

burrow into the soil, living upon plant roots. It is an insidious and very persistent pest. It can be cleared by dipping or thoroughly spraying with an organo-phosphorus compound such as Malathion or Diazitol every three weeks until clean.

Another pest which can attack Coleus is the Scale Insect. This will most certainly crawl or drop on to the plant from other infected plants nearby. They are oval in shape, flat and scale-like, and about three-sixteenths of an inch long when fully mature. In the early stages they are invisible to the naked eye. In a heavy infestation they can almost cover the stems and petioles of plants and a large area of older leaves also. Their excrement, which often goes mouldy, produces a very dirty looking plant.

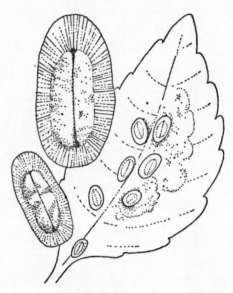

Scale Insect

The pest is controlled by using clean material at propagating time and by spraying or dipping infected plants with Malathion or Diazitol. The adults lie tightly adhered to the plant with their young underneath their bodies. Although the waxy, tough parent scale may succumb, the young, being thus protected from the remedial treatment, can survive. Several treatments of the plants are therefore necessary at intervals of about six weeks to clear up the trouble.

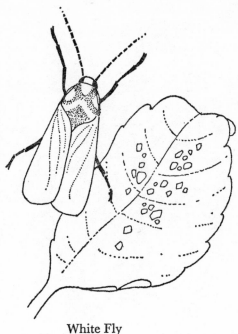

White Fly

The Greenhouse White Fly can also affect Coleus. The infection may spread from other plants inside the greenhouse at any season of the year, but during the summer months it can enter the growing quarters from infected plants in the open; sometimes weed plants serve as host. The fly can also travel down-wind for considerable distances during warm, soft weather. The creature is a tiny white fly of gnat size. It flies in a characteristic erratic zig-zag manner and usually comes to rest on the under surface of leaves where it eventually lays solitary eggs. These creatures hatch and develop into small pin-head size lozenge-shaped greeny white whiskered mounds which is the nymph stage. Ultimately, the nymph pupates and an an adult fly later emerges. A good control is to use Lindane smokes at weekly intervals. This will control the adults but not the young which have not emerged. Continue the periodic treatment until the infestation is cleaned up. If these creatures appear, endeavour to control them before they have the chance to lay eggs.

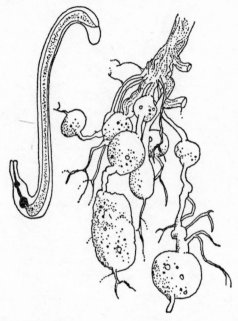

Root-knot Eelworm
This tiny eel-like worm is invisible to the naked eye and causes galls to appear on the roots, where it lives and feeds on the tissues. These galls, which appear inside the root form large swellings. Symptoms are wilting of the plants and yellowing of the leaves.

Without doubt, the worst pest of all is the Root-knot Eelworm. This description embraces more than one species of eelworm but the symptoms are the same. These eelworms are of tropical origin and are not cyst forming. Their normal mode of existence is to live inside the tissue of the plant roots. The female lays eggs, 1,000 or more at a time. These form a mass of spawn-like matter from which minute larval eelworms hatch. Some of these larvae penetrate further into the plant roots and mature there. The remainder emerge from the plant roots into the soil. If it is warm and moist they can live for several months in this larval state.

Should suitable plant root or stem tissue be at hand they will enter it and mature into adult eelworms in about thirty days time. The creatures travel through the root tissue causing swellings to occur at intervals. These may vary in the early stages from only just perceptible increases in girth to ultimately, in the later stages, large knotty galls more than an inch in diameter, the infection by now having spread to the whole root system. This causes the plant to pine and become unthrifty. As the disease is in the roots only, the plant is often discarded without the trouble being diagnosed. The contaminated debris, compost and plant pot later spread the infection to all other available plants which come into contact with it. In the beginning, the disease can be present without there being any observable symptoms. When it has progressed for a time there is no difficulty about diagnosis; the root systems becomes a whole series of swellings and galls. It is contagious and very serious.

There is no known cure for an infected plant and the only sure overall remedy is to destroy and replace, taking care that all infected specimens are disposed of in a manner that will not pass on the trouble to other plants. Adequate sterilisation by steam or suitable approved chemicals of all old roots, pots, bench coverings and the like is crucial. The effective removal of every scrap of infected material and that which has been in contact with it is imperative. Re-cover new bench tops with clean, new materials. Any crumb or smear of old, infected material could re-infect the new.

Every effort to prevent re-infection should be taken. Compost, pots, utensils etc., should be above suspicion. Steps should be taken to ensure that, if the disease has not been contained it will not spread out-of-hand. Bench tops and sand beds can be arranged in small, isolated areas; if infection is carried on to one, it will not pass to the next one. Moving plants around from one bed to another should be avoided if possible. Capillary beds will spread the disease very quickly to all plants. Potted plants, young plants and soil from outside sources should be treated with suspicion and given quarantine procedure. The placing of potted plants in individual leak-proof containers at least three inches deep is one method of isolating plants which are standing together. Tap out plants from their pots every month or so during the summer and inspect the roots. This pest has become a trouble in Britain in comparatively recent times. Aided by the increasing popularity of potted plants and the ease of their transportation, it is spreading rapidly to both commercial and amateurs' greenhouses alike, establishing itself before the grower realises that the pest has been introduced. Seeing that there is no known cure for this trouble, the best course is to avoid introducing it in the first place.

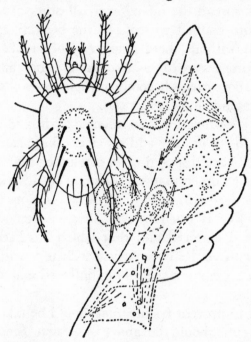

Red Spider Mite
These mites are often found in greenhouse cultivation on the underside of the leaves and feed by sucking sap. This causes the kind of mottling of the leaves which is also associated with aphides. Control of this pest is usually effected by fumigation of the greenhouse.

Sometimes, when Coleus are grown amongst other plants which are infected with Chrysanthemum eelworm, they will become

infected also. The condition causes areas of lower leaves to become discoloured or dead for no apparent reason, the grower
often not suspecting disease. Although named Chrysanthemum
eelworm, this complaint can also be seen on other glasshouse
crops, on begonias, ferns, calceolarias etc. The areas of damaged
leaf are usually delimited by major veins. Treatment would start
with a general clean up of premises and stock, the burning of
plant residue and a hygienic method of handling the whole
garden and stock.

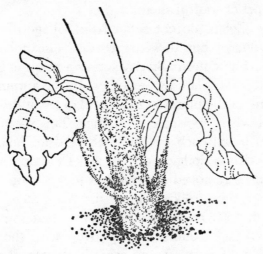

Botrytis cinerea

This disease is sometimes called 'Grey Mould' or 'Stem
Rot'. A dense, grey, furry mould appears on leaves,
stems or flowers. If the stem is attacked at the base,
the plants wilt and collapse. The disease can be controlled
and prevented from spreading by fumigating with
T.C.N.B. smokes, raising the temperature and increasing ventilation.

Coleus are sometimes infected by Spider Mites. This should
not occur if the plants are provided with the moist, humid
atmosphere in which they thrive best, but sometimes, in late
winter, when over-wintered plants have been kept dry, and
watering has been at a minimum, the mites may be noticed. The
symptoms are the disfiguration of mature leaves by pale bleached

areas of untypical colouring, but the inexperienced eye might not even notice it. The mites are very minute and a glass is needed to see them. As far as Coleus are concerned, the mites go away as the humidity rises. If an infection arises from other accompanying plants, they can be eradicated by spraying with Chlorocide or fumigating with Tedion 18. Some strains of Spider Mites originating from commercial greenhouses have evolved as a result of their having selectively resisted a long succession of acaricides. These strains are difficult to contain except with advanced types of control chemicals.

In Britain, Coleus do not suffer from foliage diseases such as rusts and mildews, but they are readily susceptible to Botrytis and soft rots. These normally develop as a result of low temperatures and excessive humidity together. In the autumn especially, dew can form on the plants at night and unless it dries off quickly rot will start where moisture is retained. This is especially liable where leaves touch each other or where dead fallen flowers or particles of debris lodge and decay. Decaying and infected leaves should be removed promptly as they are liable to infect a branch, which, in turn can infect the main stem also. Besides leaf and stem rots, root rots also occur when the temperature falls too low. This trouble usually arises with the onset of the colder weather of autumn and sometime later, the roots, commencing with the lesser ones, become dead and brown. The decay passes to the main roots and then to the main stem. Finally, the plant collapses and dies. The trouble may be started initially by the minor roots being first damaged or killed by drought or an overdose of fertiliser. Root rots can be controlled only by raising the temperature. A suitably appropriate temperature range is essential to ensure that they retain their vitality; they are then more than a match for rot-inducing organisms. If a high enough temperature cannot be maintained it must be accepted that the plants must ultimately perish.

Sometimes young plants and cuttings will decay and rot at the soil level, the young plant collapsing and falling over. This condition also is primarily a consequence of the temperature being too low. Stagnant soil or dirty infected water can introduce the organisms responsible for this condition and all water tanks should be maintained in a clean, hygienic state. Watering the young plants with Captan is useful in controlling this condition but the most effective remedy is to raise the temperature.

Index

Page numbers in italics indicate illustrations

Page numbers preceded by P. indicate colour plate facing that page

Abscission layer 80
Anthocyanins 38
Aphis 100, *101*
Apical bud *82*
Aromatic Coleus 10
Auxins 81

Bedding-out plants 98
Bibliography 27, 41, 84
Botanical terms 29
Botany of Coleus 42
Botrytis cinerea 110, *109*
Breeding 22, 39, 43, 56
Bull, William 15, 18

Carotenoids 36
Caterpillars 101, *102*
Chlorophyll 35
Chromosome number 46
Chrysanthemum eelworm 108
Classification 42-5

Climate 58, 92, 98
Coleus species :
    Coleus amboinicus 10, 52
    Coleus aromaticus 11, 32, 51
    Coleus atropurpureus Benth. 13
    Coleus barbatus 50
    Coleus bauseii 17
    Coleus bicolor 13
    Coleus blumei Benth. 10, 12, 31, 43, 46
    Coleus coppini 49
    Coleus edulis 50
    Coleus esculentus 50
    Coleus fredericii 51
    Coleus fruticosus 10
    Coleus gibsonii 15, 32
    Coleus laciniatus 13, 48
    Coleus marshallii 20
    Coleus murrayii 20
    Coleus pectinatus 31
    Coleus penzigii 57
    Coleus pictus 22
    Coleus pumilus 12, 25

Coleus rehneltianus 25
Coleus rotundifolius 11
Coleus saisonii 21
Coleus scutellarioides Benth. 48
Coleus shirensis 51
Coleus telfordii (aurea) 17, 20
Coleus thyrsoideus 24, 50
Coleus tuberosus 11, 49
Coleus veitchii 16, 32
Coleus verschaffeltii 14, 31
Coleus varieties :
  ' Autumn ' 93, *P 65*
  ' Beauty ' 93, *P 81*
  ' Brightness ' 93, *P 96*
  ' Buttermilk ' 91, 93, *P 48*
  ' Carnival ' 85, 93
  ' Crimson Ruffles ' 93, *P 80*
  ' Distinction ' 22
  ' Dunedin ' 26, 91, *P 64*, *P 81*
  ' Fantasia ' 41, 37, 40, *P 32, 64*
  ' Firebrand ' 93, *17, 33*
  ' Freckles ' 93, *P 65*
  ' Friendship ' *P 33*
  ' Glory of Luxembourg ' 87, 93,
    P 80, 97
  ' Kentish Fire ' 93, *P 17*
  ' Klondike ' 94, *P 17*
  ' Lemondrop ' 91, 94, *P 17*
  ' Lord Falmouth ' 26, 91
  ' Monarch ' 27
  ' New Hybrids ' 27, 77, *30, see*
    colour plates
  ' Paisley Shawl ' 34, 85, 94, *P 104*
  'Pastel Rainbow ' *P 81*
  ' Picturatum ' 26, 91
  ' Pineapple Beauty ' 94, *P 17, 105*
  ' Pixie ' *P 16*
  ' Prize Strain ' 27
  ' Queen Victoria ' 19
  ' Rainbow Hybrids ' 27, *P 65*
  ' Redfern ' *P 49*
  ' Rob Roy ' 26, 92

' Royal Scot ' 85, 94
' Rustic Splendour ' *P 16*
' Salmon Croton ' *P 48*
' Scarlet Ribbons ' 94, *P 16*
' Sunbeam ' 94
' Sunset ' 91
' Surprise ' 22
' Treales ' 94
' Vulcan ' *P 48*
' Walter Turner ' 85, 94, *P 105*
' White Gem ' 91
' White Fern ' *P 32*
' Winter Sun ' 94, *P 96, 104*
Colouring 31, 35, 91, *P 49*
Competitive growing 94
Compost
  Potting 61
  Seed 63
  Showing 97
  Striking 64
Croton-leaved Coleus 32, 91
Culture 58
Cuttings 24, 64, 68, 69, 70, *P 49, 64*

Didynamia 46
Diseases 100
Display of plants 91, 98, *P 104-5*

Eelworm 106

Fan shape 88
Fertiliser 61, 97
Flame Nettle 10
Flowers 50
French Nettle 10

Gas fumes, effect on Coleus 83
Genetics 39

Genus defined 44
Glycosides 38
Greenhouse layout *59, 60*
Greenhouse plants 90

Hanging baskets 91, *P 105*
Heating 59
House plants 88
Hybridisation 16, 26

Labiatae, relation to Coleus 10
Leaf :
    Botanical terms 29
    Colouring 31
    Damage 34
    Dished 34
    Dust 34
    Exhibition Cultivars *33, 37*
    Shapes 31, *30*
    Sports 34
Leaf shedding 80-3
Line breeding 26
Longevity 79
Lutein 38

Majana aurea 11
Majana rubra 48
Mealy bug 102, *103*

Named Cultivars 92
Nettle, relation to Coleus 9
'New Hybrids' 27, 77, *see colour plates*
Nitrogen, effect on colour 38, 62

Ocimum genus 44
Ocimum scutellarioides 13

Origin of Coleus 9
Over-wintering 99

Pendulous varieties 92
Pigmentation 31, 35, 91, *P 49*
    Genetic 39
Plectranthus
    Classification 42
    Relation to Coleus 9, 44
Plectranthus species :
    Plectranthus australis 57
    Plectranthus behrii 55
    Plectranthus coleoides 56
    Plectranthus esculentus 49
    Plectranthus floribundus 49
    Plectranthus fruticosus 9, 53
    Plectranthus hirtus Benth. 56
    Plectranthus örtendahlii 54
    Plectranthus scutellarioides 13
    Plectranthus ternatus Sims 49
Plectranthus 'Marginatus' 56
Potting up 74, *71-5*
Pyramid shape 85

Root-knot eelworm 106, *106*
Root rot 110
Rumphius, George Everhard 11

Scale insect 104, *104*
Seed :
    Cultivation from 24, 64, *65*
    First sales of 19
Seedlings *66, 67*
Shading of plants 66, 73, 89
Shedding of leaves 83
Shock to plants 81
Showing of Coleus 94
Slugs 102
Snails 102

115

Soft rots 110
Somatic mutation 43
Spanish thyme 52
Spider mite 109, *108*
Staging *60*
Staking plants 96
Stamens 45
Standard shape 86, *80*
Stem 35
Sterilisation after infection 107

Temperature 58, 88
Training plants 85, *77-9*
Trimming of cuttings 70
Tubers 11, 42, 49

Uses of Coleus 88

Variation 43
Varieties, named *(see also* Coleus)
    92
Veination of leaf 32

Watering 76
White fly 105, *105*
Wilting 74
Window plant 10

Xanthophylls 38